The International Hotel Industry
Sustainable Management

NOTES FOR PROFESSIONAL LIBRARIANS AND LIBRARY USERS

This is an original book title published by The Haworth Hospitality & Tourism Press™, an imprint of The Haworth Press, Inc. Unless otherwise noted in specific chapters with attribution, materials in this book have not been previously published elsewhere in any format or language.

CONSERVATION AND PRESERVATION NOTES

All books published by The Haworth Press, Inc., and its imprints are printed on certified pH neutral, acid-free book grade paper. This paper meets the minimum requirements of American National Standard for Information Sciences-Permanence of Paper for Printed Material, ANSI Z39.48-1984.

DIGITAL OBJECT IDENTIFIER (DOI) LINKING

The Haworth Press is participating in reference linking for elements of our original books. (For more information on reference linking initiatives, please consult the CrossRef Web site at www.crossref.org.) When citing an element of this book such as a chapter, include the element's Digital Object Identifier (DOI) as the last item of the reference. A Digital Object Identifier is a persistent, authoritative, and unique identifier that a publisher assigns to each element of a book. Because of its persistence, DOIs will enable The Haworth Press and other publishers to link to the element referenced, and the link will not break over time. This will be a great resource in scholarly research.

The International Hotel Industry
Sustainable Management

Timothy L. G. Lockyer

Routledge
Taylor & Francis Group

NEW YORK AND LONDON

For more information on this book or to order, visit
http://www.haworthpress.com/store/product.asp?sku=5869

or call 1-800-HAWORTH (800-429-6784) in the United States and Canada
or (607) 722-5857 outside the United States and Canada
or contact orders@HaworthPress.com

First Published by

The Haworth Hospitality & Tourism Press™, an imprint of The Haworth Press, Inc., 10 Alice Street, Binghamton, NY 13904-1580.

Transferred to Digital Printing 2010 by Routledge
270 Madison Ave, New York NY 10016
2 Park Square, Milton Park, Abingdon, Oxon, OX14 4RN

PUBLISHER'S NOTE
The development, preparation, and publication of this work has been undertaken with great care. However, the Publisher, employees, editors, and agents of The Haworth Press are not responsible for any errors contained herein or for consequences that may ensue from use of materials or information contained in this work. The Haworth Press is committed to the dissemination of ideas and information according to the highest standards of intellectual freedom and the free exchange of ideas. Statements made and opinions expressed in this publication do not necessarily reflect the views of the Publisher, Directors, management, or staff of The Haworth Press, Inc., or an endorsement by them.

Permission to use interviewees' quoted words was obtained by Timothy L. G. Lockyer.

Front cover photographs include: (left) The Ritz-Carlton, Millenia Singapore; (upper right) Sharrow Bay Hotel, England; (lower right) Turtle Bay Resort, Oahu.

Cover design by Jennifer M. Gaska.

Library of Congress Cataloging-in-Publication Data

Lockyer, Timothy L. G.
    The international hotel industry : sustainable management / Timothy L. G. Lockyer.
        p. cm.
    Includes bibliographical references.
    ISBN: 978-0-7890-3338-3 (hard : alk. paper)
    ISBN: 978-0-7890-3339-0 (soft : alk. paper)
    1. Hotel management. I. Title.
TX911.3.M27L5885 2007
647.94'068—dc22
                                                                        2007000480

CONTENTS

ABOUT THE AUTHOR

Timothy L. G. Lockyer, PhD, began his industry experience by training to become a Chef de Cuisine in a London, England, West End Hotel. From there he worked in a number of West End Hotels, including the Savoy, and then moved on to management positions in and around London. He emigrated to New Zealand in 1973 to purchase a restaurant in Wellington. After three years he left New Zealand to study and work in Hawaii, Hong Kong, and China. In 1986 he returned to New Zealand to Massey University to teach Hotel Management and while there completed a Master's of Management Studies. Three years later he went back to Wellington as Head of the School of Hospitality and Tourism Management at the Central Institute of Technology. In 1997 he became a full-time PhD student at the University of Waikato, Hamilton, New Zealand, where he completed his thesis. He is now teaching in the Department of Tourism Management at the University of Waikato and has undertaken research and published widely. He has always maintained a close working relationship with hotel management and has, over the years, undertaken consultancy and other industry-related training and activities. He has taught numerous courses in hotel management and tourism, as well as marketing, accounting, and research methodology.

Foreword

HOTEL INDUSTRY: A HISTORICAL PERSPECTIVE

Food, shelter, and clothing have been the basic needs of humankind for centuries. As humans progressed toward civilization travel became another necessity, and with travel came the need of accommodations, a "home away from home." This home away from home or an inn, motel, hotel, or lodging traces its origin back to biblical days. In the New Testament, it reveals that there was "no room in the inn" for Mary and Joseph (Prior, 1999). If one considers the dictionary meaning of an inn, motel, or hotel there is one common aspect—they all provide accommodations though there could be differences when it comes to facilities. Traditionally, inns and motels were located on highways providing accommodations, food, and drink for travelers. Prior (1999) states that Henry Ford's mass production of the Model T in 1913 led to the construction of highways and motels. It is said that the word "motel" stems from "mo" in motor and the "tel" in hotel (Prior, 1999). Architecture of motels and hotels show that usually the room door in hotels open to a corridor within the hotel building whereas the motel room door leads to an open area with vehicle parking. Motels flourished as the travel increased in the late seventeenth and eighteenth century. The growth also resulted in some competition and better expectations by the travelers, thus the start of better accommodations in the form of hotels in the late eighteenth and early nineteenth century.

Expansion of railroads in the United States in the early nineteenth century brought prosperity to the hotel industry in the 1920s. Despite some poor performance in 1930, the hotels in the United States have mostly enjoyed growth and evolution, though world wars and economic recession caused some interruption in the growth (Brown &

The International Hotel Industry: Sustainable Management
© 2007 by The Haworth Press, Inc. All rights reserved.
doi:10.1300/5869_a

Lefever, 1990). In examining the fortunes of three hotel groups in the United Kingdom, namely the Savoy Group; the London, Midland and Scottish Railway (LMSR) Company; and Trust Houses, Pope (2000) points out that each company's performance was related to the overall demand in their sector of market. All were forced to reshape and upgrade their facilities, improve marketing, and achieve cost economies (Pope, 2000). The author also points out that in the 1930s the hotel trade was much tougher as compared to the early nineteenth century and during the middle and late 1920s. Most European nations reflect historical similarities being affected by circumstances of war and economic recession at that time.

Besides the early inns and/or lodging places along the main traveling roads there were also resort destinations for holiday-makers which existed before the introduction of cars (Prior, 1999). Most of these resorts were at the seashore, the oldest example being Cape May, which is listed as a national historic landmark in the United States. Some other examples from the United States include the Lambertville Inn, Hunterdon County built in 1812 which was a stagecoach stop for U.S. presidents; Colligans Stockton Inn was built in 1710 as a private home and converted to a hotel in 1830s; 300 room Hotel Breslin, once called "The Newport of New Jersey" built in 1890. Today New Jersey has over 1,500 hotels.

The expectations of travelers and holiday-makers started to increase and the late 1940s saw the dramatic change in public awareness of hotel and restaurant cleanliness. In 1952 Kemmons Wilson took a vacation trip and found his accommodations so miserable he thought he could certainly do better himself. This gave birth to the Holiday Inn which soon became the largest chain in the world. Conrad Hilton in 1954 bought the well established Statler Hotels which go back to 1908 and operated eight well known hotels. This gave a significant boost to the Hilton empire (Brown & Lefever, 1990). In the late 1950s and 1960s the hotel industry stepped up its growth and 1960 became one of the most significant decades in the history of the lodging industry (Freeman, 1999). The continued development of interstate highways in the United States generated demand for motels and proliferation of motels continued. In 1962, the American Hotel Association had changed its name to American Hotel and Motel Association (AH&MA). By 1968, the founder of

Holiday Inns was constructing over eighty new Holiday Inns. Also around that time hotels had stared to create a brand impact which led to better service and facilities creating more competition to develop brand loyalty in the market place. In 1970 Hilton purchased controlling interests in the International and Flamingo Hotels, both in Las Vegas. Also in the 1970s the Holiday Inn moved into the gaming industry in addition to Holiday Inn Hotels and Resorts. In 1990 the Holiday Inn brand was sold to Bass PLC. The remaining Holiday Inns Inc. brands including Hampton Inn and Embassy Suites were reorganized under the name Promus. Bass has since changed its name to Six Continents (Miller, 2002). Six Continents Hotels have become known for some of the largest and widely recognized lodging brands in the world catering to different consumer levels such as Inter-Continental Hotels and resorts (founded in 1946). Crown Plaza Hotels was introduced in 1983 as a product extension of Holiday Inn and Staybridge Suites by Holiday Inn, targeting the extended stay market, was introduced in 1998 (Wagner, 2002). More and more family-oriented hotel businesses were moving to become chain hotels. Unlike the United States, the hotel industry in the United Kingdom did not have large hotel chains created by groups such as Statler and Biltmore companies. The nearest comparison could be the Trust Houses Limited which started in 1903 as Hertfordshire Public House Trust, and, by 1919, the company became the Trust House Limited.

The AH&MA summarizes as follows the time line for hotels:

- 1794—The first building constructed as a seventy-three room hotel near Trinity Church in Manhattan.
- 1826—First public restrooms in a hotel and also a barber shop, in Barnum's City Hotel, Baltimore.
- 1827—First skyscraper hotel, the six storey Adelphi, New York.
- 1829—First modern hotel with first lobby, room clerk, and separate baggage and bar rooms, Tremont House, Boston. It was also the first hotel to offer private guestrooms with locks and soap.
- 1844—First elevator installed in a hotel, Fifth Avenue Hotel, New York.
- 1882—First electric-lighted hotel the Everett Hotel, New York.
- 1883—The Sagamore Hotel on Lake George, New York, became the first hotel to have electric lights in every guestroom.

- 1904—New York St. Regis Hotel was the first to provide individually controlled heating and air-conditioning in each guestroom.
- 1924—The Motel Inn, San Luis Obispo, California, was the first roadside inn to be called a motel.
- 1927—J. Williard and Alice Marriott started A&W Root Beer Stand in Washington, DC. This was followed by a chain of Hot Shoppes and the first Marriott Hotel in 1957.
- 1930—Howard Dearing Johnson initiated the first hospitality industry franchise.
- 1934—Hotel Statler, Detroit, became the first hotel to use air-conditioning in every public room.
- 1937—The first Sheraton Hotel, the Stoneheaven, opened in Springfield, Massachusetts.
- 1938—Western Hotel, known as Westin, started in the Northwest.
- 1939—The Travelodge name was used for the first time.
- 1946—Best Western was founded by M.K. Guertin.
- 1947—New York's Roosevelt Hotel installed the first TV sets in guestrooms.
- 1952—Kemmons Wilson opened the first Holiday Inn, Memphis.
- 1953—Howard Dearing Johnson franchised his first Motor Lodge.
- 1960—Sheraton chain promised reservation confirmation in four seconds.
- 1970—Holiday Inn introduced its instant computerized reservation system.
- 1983—Ritz-Carlton Hotels launched.
- 1995—Hyatt Hotels became the first of the chains to establish a site on the Internet. (Prior, 1999)

As hotels enter the twenty-first century and embrace the technological advancements to provide better and more efficient reservation systems, improved services, and choice of luxurious amenities in rooms and public places, they also face increasing competition and challenges of a high growth business environment. For example, most higher class hotels today offer very similar facilities and amenities and it is a challenge for a hotel to portray the uniqueness of its product and position itself to be better or best. Some contemporary facilities and amenities introduced in the hotel industry include the following:

- 1965—Message lights on telephone
- 1970s—Electric cash register; POS (point of sale) system; keyless locks; and color television standard
- 1973—Free in-room movies
- 1980s—Property management system; in-room guest checkout
- 1983—In-room personal computers and call accounting system
- 1990s—On command videos (on-demand movies); interactive guest room shopping; interactive visitors guide; fax deliver; reservation from guest room for other hotels within the same organization; Internet reservations; and real estate investment trusts (Bardi, 2003)

The modern hotel industry would not have reached its current state had it not been for the dedicated contribution of its several founders. Amongst founders of the industry some important names include that of E. M. Statler who developed the chain of hotels known as Statlers. As stated earlier, in 1954, he sold the Statler Hotel chain to Conrad Hilton. Conrad Hilton became a successful hotelier after World War I, and his hotel chain had a considerable growth after World War II. Cesar Ritz was a hotelier from Switzerland whose management abilities brought him both success and fame in Europe. William Waldorf Astor and John Jacob Astor IV launched the 13-storey Waldorf Hotel in New York. Kemmons Wilson, the founder of Holiday Inns, and J. W. Marriott, who founded his empire of hotels in 1957, made great contributions to the hospitality industry. Ernest Henderson and Robert More started the Sheraton Chain in 1937. Ray Schultz, in the early 1980s, established the Hampton Inn hotels, which was associated with Holiday Inn Corporation (Bardi, 2003). The history of hotels is full of interesting founders and ever-evolving concepts which have kept improving the operational services and variety of products that hotels offer today. It is worth stating here that a sound understanding of operations management and current techniques have facilitated the growth and development of the industry.

Dr. Asad Mohsin
Department of Tourism and Hospitality Management,
The University of Waikato,
New Zealand

REFERENCES

Bardi, J.A. (2003). *Hotel front office management* (3rd ed.). NJ: John Wiley & Sons.

Brown, T.E., & Lefever, M.M. (1990). A 50-year renaissance: The hotel industry from 1039 to 1989. *Cornell Hotel and Restaurant Administration Quarterly, 31*(1), 18-25.

Freeman, T. (1999). The 1960s: Prosperity spurs malls, hotels in technicolor dream. *National Real Estate Investor, 41*(11), 28.

Miller, K. (2002). Industry first, *Memphis Business Journal, 24*(10), 19.

Pope, R. (2000). A consumer service in interwar Britain: The hotel trade. *Business History Review, 74*(4), 657-683.

Prior, J.T. (1999). Hotels: The lodging industry keeps up with times. *New Jersey Business, 45*(10), 62.

Wagner, G. (2002). Holiday Inn 50. *Lodging Hospitality, 58*(11), 21-29.

Preface

There are many good books available internationally about the hospitality industry; these tend to fall into two categories: those that are of an introductory nature or give an overview of the industry and those that take a specific disciplinary approach (marketing, human resource, accounting, and so on). Very often the texts are geographically oriented (United States or Europe). This book takes a different approach; it is international, interdisciplinary, and questioning. To quote Nash Nasihin Ali, general manager, Mutiara Hotel, Johor, Malaysia, "Hotel management now is complex, you have to wear many hats and play many roles." The very definition of the hotel industry is one that signifies an international market. A manager in London is just as likely to find himself/herself working in New York, Beijing, or Paris. As we look at the management issues in these different environments, it is interesting to note how common the problems are internationally, for example, yield management is just as much a concern in London as it is in Beijing. However, although the problems are the same in many areas there are also very striking differences and issues that managers need to be aware of in the complex environment in which they work. Each issue has to be considered in light of the surrounding elements of that environment, which often changes the required action.

A prime objective of this book is to make sure that this international perspective is represented. It is impossible to cover every single issue in each country, but it is possible to give a reasonable example of some of the management problems impacting different regions of the world.

In order to provide current and real examples of issues facing hotel management today, interviews were conducted in many countries with senior managers in a variety of different hotels, and actual quo-

The International Hotel Industry: Sustainable Management
© 2007 by The Haworth Press, Inc. All rights reserved.
doi:10.1300/5869_b

tations from these interviews are a key component of this book. The interviews were transcribed as accurately as possible, slightly modified at times to apply to a specific situation, and give fascinating and inspirational information and insight to the reader. They are invaluable and are used to give this book richness of perspective for students and those involved in the international hotel industry. The interviews were undertaken with hotel general managers and sometimes included other key personnel in the hotel from specific departments, which helped to give the discussion an additional perspective.

The industry research makes the theory offered in the book timely and relevant to the current key topics in the hotel industry. The interviews are not presented as a "how to" type of discussion, but more to help identify the issues and how management deals with them, and to give the reader the opportunity to think about some of the topics raised, with encouragement to work through and consider how they as managers might deal with the situations presented.

Each major chapter in the book follows a similar pattern, and has been developed to stimulate discussion and consideration of the various areas discussed. The chapters go from a general introduction, presentation of theory, through a discussion of the issues in available literature with the inclusion of interview data. The chapters also include questions for consideration, a variety of case studies and, of particular importance, thought-provoking questions about the topics covered in the chapter.

This book is based on the identified issues facing international hotel managers. In a formal educational environment it is strongly recommended that students read through the text before attending the classes and that the issues covered are given relevance by comparing local and pertinent issues. This text is not intended as a definitive work, but more to stimulate discussion and to develop the ability to understand the management decision making process. As a result it is recommended that at least some of the references are followed to give additional depth to the discussion. Some of the examples may seem strange and quite alien to particular groups of students, but the value of them is that the student becomes aware of what is happening outside their realm of immediate understanding of the hotel industry.

This book is designed to be used at many levels, and could in theory be used for all levels from beginners through students pursuing their masters'. Many of the subject areas covered in this book are dealt with as separate courses (human resource management, marketing etc.). This book could be of great value for use in a keystone course, to bring all the areas together.

Part of the market for this book is the educational purpose, but this is by no means its only use. It is also aimed at those currently employed or thinking of employment in the industry.

Both positives and negatives have been raised in this book—often, we tend to look at the positive implications but to gain a balanced view, the negatives are also important. Readers are encouraged to look at the negatives as appropriate, and analyze the implications of decisions to be made. What may be seen as positive in one environment may not be seen in the same light in another environment.

Very often, after completion of the traditional introductory type courses, students tend to specialize in specific disciplines, in areas such as reservations, housekeeping, finance, marketing, human resources. Although each of these is of immense importance, often the student's study becomes somewhat compartmentalized into the disciplines being covered and as a result the student has difficulty in perceiving the place of that discipline in the "whole." For clarity, the chapters in this book deal with distinct areas: they should not be considered in isolation—in fact, within the actual running of a hotel, they overlap and intermingle. For example, empowerment influences yield management, human resource policies influence marketing, and so on. The reader of this book is encouraged to take a holistic view of the issues, to "step back" and consider how the different issues impact one another, in particular consider issues pertaining to the sustainability of the business, and how this may influence the management decision making process.

The book has been tested for three semesters in graduate classes. The students report that they find the book interesting, logical, and challenging. The students are assigned to read a chapter, undertake additional research, and be ready to discuss the issues raised in the respective chapter. Since our graduate classes run for a four-hour period, there is sufficient material for in-depth discussion. The discussion normally starts by having one or two students give an overview of the chapter; this is then followed by students being asked to discuss and elaborate on the individual topics with the facilitator guiding the discussion. The class is then split into groups with each of the "discussion" questions assigned to the groups for them to present and share their comments (note—some of these have to be assigned previously as they require additional research). Finally, the case studies are discussed as a group. At the end of the class the students have to complete a written summary of the chapter, giving their views of what was most important and interesting along with significant additional literature and other research to support their views. The key assessment for the course is a project where the students develop a proposal for a hotel or resort as realistically as possible. This can be anything from backpacking to an exclusive hotel. In the project each of the issues in the book must be covered and placed in the right context.

Acknowledgments

This book contains a series of interviews. Managers in various countries were contacted and agreed to be interviewed. The interviews were recorded and transcribed as accurately as possible, although minor changes were made to convert the spoken word into written form. Where any questions were deemed to be inappropriate or the answers may have been sensitive to the running of the hotel or the chain, managers were at liberty to decline to answer. When a manager did not wish to answer the question, those wishes were accepted and the interview moved on to other areas. In the interviews, all participants agreed to allow quotes to be compiled for the benefit of readers of the book. At the copyediting stage of preparation, every effort was made to contact the participants and where contact was made final permission to print was given.

Those interviewed, whose quotations appear in the text, are:

Nash Nasihin Ali, general manager, Mutiara Hotel, Johor, Malaysia

Antonio R. Alvarez, director, Hotel Beatriz Palace, Fuengirola, Spain

S. M. Azmat, senior vice president, Jaypee Palace Hotel, Agra, India

Luis C. Barrios, general manager, Hacienda Hotel Old Town, San Diego, USA

Abid Butt, managing director, Turtle Bay Resort, Hawaii, USA

Chris Collier, CEO, Cumbria Tourist Board, Cumbria, England

Rafael de la Fuente, director gerente, Escuela de Hosteleria, Benalmedena Pueblo, Spain

Bruce Fery, general manager, Grand America, Salt Lake City, USA

Octavio Gamarra, general manager; Anton Kilayko, director public relations; Estelita Sebeto, executive assistant; Robert

The International Hotel Industry: Sustainable Management
© 2007 by The Haworth Press, Inc. All rights reserved.
doi:10.1300/5869_c

Lagerway, hotel manager; William Chu, director, revenue strategy

Belinda Goh, director, sales and marketing; Patsy Chan, director, communications; Daisy Wong, director, human resources, Kowloon Shangri-La, Hong Kong

Nick Hanson, general manager, Sharrow Bay, Penrith, Engalnd

Terry Holmes, executive director, The Stafford, London, England

Lynette Lesslar, director, training and development, Ritz-Carlton Millenia, Singapore

Christopher Norton, general manager, Four Seasons, Singapore

Steve Pagano, hotel manager, Marriott Hotel & Marina, San Diego, USA

Peter Pollmeier, general manager; David Lim, executive assistant manager food and beverage; Ralph Wong, rooms division, Crowne Plaza, Shenzen, China

P. S. Ramdas, managing director, Tourist Home (Pvt.) Ltd., Egmore, India

Simon Rogan, manager, L'Enclume, Cartmel, England

Linda Wan, general manager, Hotel Crescent Court, Dallas, USA

Vijay Wanchoo, general manager, corporate planning, Fortune Park Hotels, New Delhi, India

Sincere appreciation is expressed to these individuals for their generous sharing of time and experience, which has greatly enriched this work.

Introduction:
Characteristics of the Hotel Industry

Hotels are part of what is referred to as the service industry; the word service is widely used to denote industry sectors that "do things for you. They don't make things" (Silvestro & Johnston, 1990, p. 206). Service includes organizations which meet the needs of society, such as "health service," "banking," "entertainment," and "civil services" (Johns, 1999). As a result of increasing affluence and leisure time, a large majority of western countries have become service economies (Kotler, Bowen, & Makens, 1996). Services have specific characteristics which are important when analyzing these types of industries, namely intangibility, inseparability, variability, and perishability.

INTANGIBILITY

Services are frequently described as intangible as their output is viewed as an activity, rather than a tangible object (Johns, 1999). Unlike physical products, the service components in a hotel cannot be seen, tasted, felt, heard, or smelt before they are purchased. As a result the customer can neither properly evaluate nor sample prior to purchase (Blois, 1983). On researching the factors that affect hotel occupancy, this intangibility makes the exercise more complex.

As illustrated by Kotler, Bowen, and Makens (1996, p. 82), "Members of a hotel sales force cannot take a hotel room with them on a sales call, in fact do not sell a room; instead they sell the right to use a room for a specific period of time." On completion of their stay in a hotel the guest has nothing to show for that purchase, but a receipt. When they leave they are not entirely empty-handed—they take with

The International Hotel Industry: Sustainable Management
© 2007 by The Haworth Press, Inc. All rights reserved.
doi:10.1300/5869_01

them the memories of the experience, which can be shared with other people (Lewis & Chambers, 1989). In an attempt to reduce the amount of uncertainty that is felt by guests over the intangibility, they look for tangible evidence that will provide information on which there can be built greater confidence in the purchase decision (Saleh & Ryan, 1992). A lot of the effort on behalf of the hotel goes into such areas as the front desk and reception, as these are often the first points of contact.

INSEPARABILITY

In many hotel transactions the service provider and the guest must be present for the transaction to take place (Kotler, Bowen, & Makens, 1996). The customer-employee contact is also part of the product. Although the food in a restaurant might be outstanding, if the person serving the food does not have a good attitude or gives inappropriate service the customer will not be satisfied with the experience. Inseparability also means that the customer is also a part of the product. For example, one group of customers can have a significant impact on another group by being loud and boisterous or in some other way affecting the other customers. There is a requirement also for employees to understand cultural differences and the way in which this impacts the customer-employee interaction (Morrison, 1989).

VARIABILITY

Service offered may be subject to high levels of variability. The quality has a lot to do with who, where, and when the service is provided. The fluctuating demand in hotels makes it difficult on many occasions, such as peak periods, to control the quality of service that would be expected at other times (Kotler, Bowen, & Makens, 1996). Staff training usually seeks to reduce this level of variability as far as possible (Mullins, 1992), but often the variability is caused by factors which are not controllable.

PERISHABILITY

The service industry's final output is an intangible and ephemeral commodity in which the final output is not a good/material (Gershuny & Miles, 1983). Christopher, McDonald, and Wills (1980) state that service industries are distinct because the product is one that produces a series of benefits, but the benefits cannot be stored (other than in the memory). For example, if a hotel room is not sold on any particular night it cannot be stored in inventory and sold the following night. The revenue from the sale of that room is lost forever and as a result the product offered by a hotel is considered to be perishable (Mullins, 1993).

Each of these issues indicate the characteristics in which the hotel industry operates and each has an impact on the factors that affect occupancy. The level of occupancy is important because a hotel comprises space in the form of guest rooms and other areas. The development of these areas has a cost. Those investing in the development of a hotel have an expectation of the highest possible return on their investment. One way of maximizing this return is to have the highest occupancy within the hotel, at the highest possible price per occupied area (Coltman, 1994).

These characteristics, which of themselves are not unique to hotel management, outline a particular environment in which hotels operate. These characteristics include physiological and psychological, along with a host of other considerations, as suggested by Nailon (1982, pp. 139-140):

1. Satisfying basic psychological needs
2. Satisfying identity, status, security
3. Customer satisfaction is individual
4. Satisfaction is transient
5. Customer need is immediate
6. Customers influence other customers
7. Customer is part of product and therefore product is uncontrollable
8. Customer interaction is of short duration
9. Staff-customer relations are personal

10. Customer expectations can trigger ambiguity
11. Product is transient: a meal or bed cannot be stored (1982, pp. 139-140)

This paints a picture of the characteristics of an industry that is heavily reliant on the interaction between the guest and the employees of a hotel, and of a product that is difficult to quantify and measure (Hope & Mühlemann, 1997; King, 1986). The major characteristic, which is common in almost all situations, is that the product offered by hotels makes them part of the service sector (Buttle, 1986).

In many parts of the world the occupancy of the rooms contributes the majority of revenue and profit for a hotel. Because the marginal cost of selling a room is relatively low and room sales lead to other sales in the hotel's other facilities such as restaurants and bars, it is important that the number of occupied rooms is maximized (Chin, Barney, & O'Sullivan, 1995). Hotels enjoying profitability are those with the right mix of product, quality, price, and service (Sheridan, 1995).

The return on the investment is important to a hotel. The development of a hotel involves a large investment in fixed costs (McEvoy, 1997). The evaluation of the use of this investment comes through the return on the hotel's facilities. There is a close relationship between operating efficiency of a hotel and the return on investment as expressed in its financial statements (McEvoy, 1997). Occupancy rate is a way of measuring the success or failure in the utilization of hotel rooms. This is defined as the number of rooms occupied on any particular night divided by the number of rooms available to be let (Brymer, 1988). The number of rooms available is used as often not all the rooms in an establishment can be let because of refurbishment, maintenance, and lack of ability to clean the room in time. The result of this is the occupancy percentage for that particular night. In the United States, in 1993 there was an average occupancy across the whole market of 64 percent (Rice, 1993).

While occupancy rate is one of the measures of hotel success there are a number of other ways to measure performance. These include the number of occupied rooms, the average room rate, and comparing actual to budgeted revenue (Orkin, 1988). Management take different approaches to optimizing their return. Reduced to essentials, hotels are in the business of generating revenue from space. Management's principal function is to produce the best possible return on the space available (Jeffrey & Hubbard, 1994). The need to fill the space at the right price "has possibly caused managers to forget that what they perceive (as the right price) . . . may not be seen in the same light by their customers" (Huyton, Evans, & Ingold, 1997).

The traditional focus of hotel operations and management has been tactical and departmental. As argued by Hum (1997), most of the literature is dedicated to describing either the general management of the overall hotel or the specific techniques and tools for a particular department such as marketing, human resource management, and corporate strategy, along with the operational areas such as food and beverage and housekeeping. This reductionist view, whereby the organization is seen as the mechanical sum of departments or functional areas (Gull, 1995), is illustrated when looking at the structure of many hotels where there are departments for food and beverage with a subsection of food production and food service, housekeeping, marketing, and so on. The reductionist view of a hotel is also reflected in research undertaken into the industry in specific disciplines (Jones, 1993). Each different discipline or school of thought has its own root metaphor for the understanding of reality (Morgan, 1980). As stated by Gull (1995, p. 17):

> The properties of an organization are not reducible to the properties of the individual departments or functional areas. An understanding of the organization cannot come from an in-depth analysis of each functional area; such an approach will only lead to misunderstanding and errors in judgment.

The organizational structure of hotels has flattened in recent years, especially with the introduction of total quality management (TQM) principles and practices. Even with this flattening of the organization structure there is still clear differentiation between different positions within hotel organizations (Lockyer, 1993). As a result, a hotel is often viewed as a group of separate revenue generating operations or departments, and not as a whole operation interacting internally and externally to the environment in which it exists.

In the hotel model described there is emphasis on the success of in-dividual departments and their ability to return an income on their op-eration, which is referred to as functional management (Jones & Pizam, 1993). Each department or area of the hotel has its own opera-tional budget, with expected income and expenditure (Coltman, 1994). The operations management approach views every operation as a series of steps or stages (Jones & Lockwood, 1989). In this kind of model emphasis is given to the way in which the manager influences the workforce and the outcome of the operation. Therefore each indi-vidual department, such as a restaurant or a bar, has an impact on the success of the hotel. This approach to managing a hotel considers the individual department and does not take into account the influence that each department has on the others and the impact of external factors.

In contrast to this reductionist approach to hotel management, some have argued that practice should be interdisciplinary (Benton, 1976; Slattery, 1983; Littlejohn, 1990). This management approach is defined as "in-between disciplines" (Kilburn, 1990). A hotel is an interdisciplinary environment (Buckley & Chapman, 1996) where different departments show convergence, which is achieved despite diversity (Birts et al., 1997) and involves consideration of the overall hotel and the factors that impact it.

The settings in which hotel management takes place are diverse in terms of geographic location, ownership structure of the organization, level of service and product provided, and other external and inter-nal factors. As a result, hotel research draws on multiple disciplines in management as well as related fields in the behavioral and social sciences. As Lashley (1998, p. 295) advocates:

> traditional research that tends to focus on single independent variables that will supposedly alter a dependent variable, does not recognize the interdependence of inter-functional and inter-factorial influences in hospitality management.

Because of the diversity of hotels and the influences on them as suggested by Jones and Lockwood (1989), this approach to the cur-rent research is most appropriate (Roper & Brookes, 1999). Thus, due to the diverse industry setting of hotels, an interdisciplinary approach to the study of hotel occupancy is called for, so that the research can cover the many factors influencing occupancy, and is not restricted to considering individual discipline related factors such as marketing and human resource.

REFERENCES

Benton, D.A. (1976). Management and effectiveness measures for interdisciplinary research. *SRA Journal*, Spring, 37-45.

Birts, A., McAulay, L., Pitt, M., et al. (1997). The expertise of finance and accountancy: An interdisciplinary study. *British Journal of Management, 8*(1), 75-84.

Blois, K. (1983). Service marketing—Assertion or asset. *Service Industries Journal, 3*(2), 113-120.

Brymer, R.A. (1988). *Introduction to Hotel and restaurant management*. IA: Kendall/Hunt Publishing Company.

Buckley, P.J., & Chapman, M. (1996). Theory and method in international business research. *International Business Review, 5*(3), 233-246.

Buttle, F. (1986). *Hotel and food service marketing*. London: Holt, Rinehart and Winston.

Chin, J., Barney, W., & O'Sullivan, H. (1995). *Hotels, an introductory accounting and auditing guide*. Central Milton, KS: Accounting Books.

Christopher, M., McDonald, M., & Wills, G. (1980). *Introducing marketing*. London: Pan Books.

Coltman, M.M. (1994). *Hospitality management accounting*. New York: Van Nostrand Reinhold.

Gershuny, J.I., & Miles, I.D. (1983). *The new service economy*. London: Frances Printer.

Gull, G.A. (1995). In search of TQM success. *Executive Excellence, 12*(7), 17-18.

Hope, C., & Mühlemann, A. (1997). *Service operations management*. London: Prentice Hall.

Hum, S.H. (1997). Strategic hotel operations: Some lessons from strategic manufacturing. *International Journal of Contemporary Hospitality Management, 9*(4), 176-179.

Huyton, J., Evans, P., & Ingold (1997). The legal and moral issues surrounding the practise of yield management. *International Journal of Contemporary Hospitality Management, 9*(2), 84-87.

Jeffrey, D., & Hubbard, N.J. (1994). A model of hotel occupancy performance for monitoring and marketing in the hotel industry. *International Journal of Hospitality Management, 13*(1), 57-71.

Johns, N. (1999). What is this thing called service? *European Journal of Marketing, 33*(9/10), 958-973.

Jones, P. (1993). Operations management issues. In P. Jones, & A. Pizam (Eds.), *The international hospitality industry: Organisational and operational Issues* (pp. 135-151). New York: John Wiley & Sons.

Jones, P., & Lockwood, A. (1989). *The management of hotel operations*. London: Cassell.

Jones, P., & Pizam, A. (1993). *The international hospitality industry: Organisational and operational Issues*. New York: John Wiley & Sons.

Kilburn, K.D. (1990). An effective interdisciplinary research team. *R & D Management, 20*(2), 131-139.

King, C.A. (1986). New look at quality assurance. In R.C. Lewis (Ed.), *The Practice of Hospitality Management II*, (pp. 27-35). London: AVI Publishing Co.

Kotler, P., Bowen, J., & Makens, J. (1996). *Marketing for hospitality and tourism*. London: Prentice-Hall International (UK) Limited.

Lashley, C. (1998). *Action research: An essential tool for hospitality management education?* 7th Annual CHME Hospitality Research Conference, Kelvin Conference Centre, Glasgow, 15-16 April, 294-310. In Roper, A., & Brookes, M. (1999). Theory and reality of interdisciplinary research. *International Journal of Contemporary Hospitality Management, 11*(4), 174-179.

Lewis, R.C., & Chambers, R.E. (1989). *Marketing leadership in hospitality*. New York: Van Nostrand Reinhold.

Littlejohn, D. (1990). Hospitality research: Philosophies and progress. In R. Teare, L. Moutinho, & N. Morgan, (Eds.), *Managing and marketing services in the 1990s*. London: Cassell Education Ltd.

Lockyer, T. (1993). *Total quality management in the hospitality industry, Proceedings*. PATA Conference Singapore.

McEvoy, B.J. (1997). Integrating operational and financial perspectives using yield management techniques: an add-on matrix model. *International Journal of Contemporary Hospitality Management, 9*(2), 60-66.

Morgan, G. (1980). Paradigms, metaphors, and puzzle solving in organization theory. *Administrative Science Quarterly, 25*(4), 605-622.

Morrison, A. (1989). *Hospitality and travel marketing*. New York: Delmar Publishing Inc.

Mullins, L.J. (1992). *Hospitality management: A human resources approach*. London: Pitman Publishing.

Mullins, L.J. (1993). The hotel and the open system model of organisational analysis. *The Service Industry Journal, 13*(1), 1-16.

Nailon, P. (1982). Theory in hospitality management. *International Journal of Hhospitality Management, 1*(3), 139-140.

Orkin, E.B. (1988). Boosting your bottom line with yield management. *Cornell Hotel and Restaurant Administration Quarterly, 28*(4), 52-56.

Rice, F. (1993, October 4). Why hotel rates won't take off—yet. *Fortune, 128*(8), 124-127.

Roper, A., & Brookes, M. (1999). Theory and reality of interdisciplinary research. *International Journal of Contemporary Hospitality Management, 11*(4), 174-179.

Saleh, F., & Ryan, C. (1992). Client perceptions of hotels, a multi-attribute approach. *Tourism Management*, (June), 163-168.

Sheridan, M. (1995). The hospitality market: 180-degree turnaround has left the hotel industry in economic bliss. *National Real Estate Investor, 37*(13), 22-28.

Silvestro, R., & Johnston, R. (1990). The determinants of service quality—enhancing and hygiene factors. *Proceedings of the QUIS II Symposium*, St John's University, New York.

Slattery, P. (1983). Social scientific methodology and hospitality management. *International Journal of Hospitality Management, 2*(1), 9-14.

Chapter 1

Location

Location, Location, Location!

CHAPTER OBJECTIVES

On completion of this chapter the reader will understand:

- the influence of location on occupancy
- the relationship between room rate and location
- the impact of guest willingness to travel and hotel location
- the relationship between location and staffing issues
- the impact of the changing environment and a hotel's location
- the relationship between location and hotel development
- the impact of location on supply of goods and services

Key Word Definitions

agglomeration: The potential of the system for particle attraction and adhesion (i.e., cluster).

commodification: To turn into or treat as a commodity; make commercial.

distance decay: The willingness of people to travel to an attraction or event.

environmental scanning: Constantly monitoring all changes and developments external to the hotel.

The International Hotel Industry: Sustainable Management
© 2007 by The Haworth Press, Inc. All rights reserved.
doi:10.1300/5869_02

FIT: A free and independent traveler.

Greenfield site: A piece of usually semi-rural property that is undeveloped except for agricultural use, especially one considered as a site for expanding urban development, in this case a hotel.

hedonic: Of, relating to, or marked by pleasure.

purpose location: The reason or purpose for the guest's stay in the hotel.

rack rate: Comes from a manual hotel reservation system (the Witney System) where the amount to be charged for rooms was stored in a rack.

room rate: The amount charged for a room in a hotel.

Chapter Review

The location of a hotel is often referred to as the only attribute that cannot be changed, at least in the short term. Where a hotel is situated has significant impacts on the market that is attracted and the profitability of the establishment, for example, the willingness of guests to travel, the need of the guest to be near an attraction/event or business meeting, the room rate, staffing and supplies, and even the "life expectancy" of the hotel. Using location to the best advantage is an important issue for hotel management, as is keeping a watchful eye on how the location of the property is changing in order to respond appropriately to those changes. Location also has an impact on the local environment with issues such as traffic congestion, visual impact, resource use, and pollution. Hotel management needs to be constantly aware of the location of the property, and not simply take it as something they can do nothing about. Planning must include all stakeholders to ensure that location is used to the best advantage.

INTRODUCTION TO THEORY: LOCATION

It is commonly asserted that the three most important attributes that a hotel can offer are location, location, and location; a phrase that is freely used by hotel marketers and hotel real estate agents (Bull, 1994). A good location is important to the sustainable management of a hotel. Even excellent marketing cannot overcome the problems inherent in an inferior location (Moutinho & Paton, 1991). The location of the hotel is the only factor of the product that is completely fixed in the short term (Bull, 1994). Location is a complex mixture of attributes, for example, where location close to city areas might be seen as an advantage to some, surrounding characteristics such as noise and congestion may be seen as a disadvantage and the hotel's use of natural resources may have impacts on the community as a whole. A contrasting view is shown by the following (Cartmel is a very small village located in the Lake District, approximately 200 miles from London).

> *This hotel is located in a very isolated region—what impact do you think the location has on your business?*
>
> I am a firm believer it's what you do, it doesn't matter where you are. I think that people will travel eventually and the business will gradually build up. We knew we couldn't rely on the local clientele (without being too rude—the local population don't really understand the type of things we do here. They haven't quite grasped the "you get what you pay for" scenario). The location didn't really come into it. The thing that attracted me was basically the building. I was confident with the product that we had; that with the public relations structure we had, we were going to get people coming to us.
>
> (Simon Rogan, Manager, L'Enclume, Cartmel, Cumbria, England)

As location is a fixed attribute, it has to be considered along with many other influencing factors. For example, location directly impacts room rate, also influencing staffing and service quality, the supply of goods and services, the use of natural resources, and pollution. Therefore, the location of a hotel cannot be considered in isolation from other factors, it must be considered on a strategic level with full awareness of the factors that the hotel's location are influenced by and have influence over.

This chapter will consider the major issues that management need to take into account in relation to location. The first of these is room rate, as it has arguably the largest direct impact on the hotel's profitability. Although in a later chapter the question of room rate is discussed under the heading of yield management, room rate must also be looked at in relation to location.

LOCATION AND ROOM RATE

The development of a new hotel is often undertaken in a location that is close to the reason for the guest's stay in the hotel. As an example, business guests may desire to be located close to meetings and other business necessities. Therefore, hotels targeting business trade will be located accordingly. Likewise, this applies to tourists who may wish to be close to a particular scenic or appealing form of attraction. These two examples are not entirely different, in that the urban tourist cities provide the visitor with a variety of historical associations such as buildings and monuments, castles, cathedrals, museums, galleries, orchestras, and amusements, while on the other hand, a scenic region away from major commercial areas can provide the business guest the opportunity to hold meetings and conventions in a more relaxed, congenial atmosphere. The Crowne Plaza is located about twenty minutes by taxi from the main downtown area. As is illustrated in the following extract, there are advantages to this location.

How does your location influence occupancy?

Our location is right. We are quite a bit out of town and we benefit because downtown hotels have a problem with crime, prostitution, and the traffic is a mess.

(Peter Pollmeier, General Manager,
Crowne Plaza, Shenzhen, China)

A factor that can have a direct influence on the room rate that a hotel can charge is the distance that it is from what can be considered the "purpose location." This is applicable for all guests staying in a hotel and examples can be seen in many places around the world. For example, a family wishing to visit Disneyland in Anaheim, California, have a number of choices: do they stay in a hotel close to, or at Disneyland and maybe pay a premium; or stay further away at an establishment with a lower room rate. The answer to this question can directly influence demand and the amount that a hotel charges (Lockyer, 2005). Research conducted by Arbel and Pizam (1977) endeavored to determine what distance tourists were prepared to travel to visit attractions. Their research was carried out among 300 foreign English-speaking tourists who spent at least a one-night stay in Israel in the

Tel Aviv metropolitan region. During the collection of the data there was no reference to price made. It was assumed that regular public transport was available at a reasonable cost.

Referred to as a distance decay, results showed that where there is up to twenty minutes traveling time there is a high willingness (37.1 percent) to travel from the accommodation in which the tourist is staying to visit attractions, but once this rises to a travel time of thirty minutes or more, the willingness to travel decreases considerably, to 14.9 percent. For tourists the willingness to travel influences their choice of accommodations. Returning to the example of Disneyland, being farther away from Disneyland may well reduce the amount that is charged by an accommodation provider, but this reduction needs to be considered along with the additional traveling time that is required and the cost of such travel.

The trend in many parts of the world is the growing availability of leisure time. This is impacting the number of holidays people are taking and their travel patterns.

What influence does the changing holiday pattern have on your hotel?

People are saying, I have forty-seven days holiday per year. So we are going to have four holidays a year. Easter—take seven days, summer take three weeks, Christmas take one week plus the national festivals and national days like long week ends. If they go to Majorca, it takes three hours in a plane then one hour in a bus. When you have one week you don't want to go too far away. So they have a car and are from perhaps Granada, Cordova, Seville, Gibraltar—areas where they have a lot of people working in factories, fairly highly paid. So they choose a hotel that is maybe only two hours away—for a short holiday they want to stay near.

(Toni Alvarez, Director,
Hotel Beatriz Palace, Fuengirola, Spain)

An interesting example was identified in research by Guseman (1988) who reported on hotel location and an aging population. As people around the world live longer coupled with the availability of a growing number of medical treatments that can improve the quality of life, there is also a growing need for visits to medical facilities and accommodation close to medical facilities (Guseman, 1988). This change in demand can influence the room rate charged by current properties in the vicinity and also act as an indicator for the need of further development of hotels in such locations.

Research into the analysis that guests undertake in the selection of room rate they are willing to pay and purpose location (Lockyer, 2005) has revealed additional insight. For example, if the need arises at short notice to visit or to be with someone in hospital, then the location becomes far more important than the amount paid for accommodations, all other things being equal. On the other hand, a person planning well in advance for a vacation or visit for some other event or attraction may place a much higher price on the list of requirements. An example of the direct relationship between room rate and location is a complex decision-making process on the part of the prospective guest. An attempt to bring a quantifiable relationship between the room rate and location question is suggested by Bull (1994, p. 12), where a hedonic price model is provided indicating the various parts of the location and how these influence the pricing strategy of the hotel

$$P \text{ sub } Mi = P(A \text{ sub } 1i, A \text{ sub } 2i \ldots A \text{ sub } ni)$$

where P sub Mi = the price (room rate) of a standard room in motel I and A sub 1i to A sub ni are the quantities of attributes A sub 1 to A sub n possessed by motel i.

Although the research by Bull (1994, p. 12) was limited in its scope it does indicate how the various attributes of a property come together to influence the room rate. This model does not take into consideration factors such as the rating of the property. In many locations worldwide star rating of accommodations is done on a five or six point rating scale, with the higher the number of stars the higher the rating of the property. Although such systems are often very regimented in their approach to the allocation of grades (e.g., Do the front office staff wear name badges, yes or no?), there is research evidence that such rating of a property does increase the amount guests are willing to pay. However, such rating systems rarely take into consideration the purpose location.

Although some properties may predominantly develop a single-use market such as a business hotel, others may target a number of different markets at the same time. For example, in Wellington,

New Zealand, the city hotels during the normal business week charge quite different room rates than during the weekend, when the rate charged may be as much as half of that which is charged during the week. The high fixed cost of development of a hotel continues if the rooms are occupied or not. Although during the weekend the hotels in Wellington may not make the return on a particular room that can be made during the weekdays and may not cover all costs, this room rate charging decision represents an effort on the part of management to cover all variable costs and to contribute toward fixed costs (Jagels & Coltman, 2004).

THE CHANGING HOTEL LOCATION

Although the hotel location is fixed, the surrounding area may go through a process of change. Consideration of the life expectancy of a hotel can aid in the formulation of alternative strategies for the hotel so that as the location changes there is a clear plan ahead (Plog, 2001). This requires a long-term view.

A hotel's survival is linked directly to the location in which it is situated. Over a period of time, a location's popularity with potential guests can change. The positioning of a hotel rests on two main factors: (1) the true qualities of a location and (2) its perception in the eyes of the guest.

The following interview describes a situation where a property once having high occupancy has been greatly influenced by the changing surroundings.

How have the changes in the local area where you are situated impacted upon your business?

The city is changing its character; as the city moves to the south the concentration of businesses are moving there also. The train station used to be in the city center and that is where the original development started (with this hotel located just across the road from the main station). Madras (now Chennai) central was where there was a concentration of hotels. At one time the train used to just come here, but now with the development, passengers have the facility of getting off the train before arriving at this central station. There were no hotels at the other places previously but now hotels have been built in the other areas, around the new stations so people can get out depending on where their work and their business is and find accommodation close by. We also used to have buses come in from all over the south of India and they used to start and terminate in this area. Because of congestion within the city they built a huge terminal at the outskirts of the city and they banned buses coming into the city. Five years ago we had an occupancy rate of 90 percent and today it is 65 percent. During this time, the average room rate has also decreased.

(P. S. Ramdas, Managing Director,
Tourist Home [Pvt.] Ltd, Egmore, Chennai, India)

In this example a once thriving hotel with an excellent location giving a good return on the investment has become a property with little return on the investment, and with little opportunity of being able to be sold for a reasonable amount. If the hotel had been sold at its prime, perhaps five years ago, it would have received an excellent return on the investment, but due to the change in location, its value is now greatly diminished.

What about if you were to sell the property?

The occupancy has declined so much it is better to keep it. Because of the deterioration of the local surrounds because of the movement south of the city, I have been trying to think what else the building could be used for. But even converted into offices, it is in a poor location.

(P. S. Ramdas, Managing Director,
Tourist Home [Pvt.] Ltd, Egmore, Chennai, India)

A great deal has been written about destinations having a life cycle. Butler (1980) suggested that a tourist destination goes through a number of stages from "birth" to "maturity" and finally to "old age" and "decline." As has been demonstrated in a number of research projects, the model as proposed by Butler (1980) is not applicable to all destinations and, in fact, can be misleading in the case of many destinations, for example, the Pacific islands (Dexter, 1992). What is of importance is the realization that destinations do go through some form of life cycle and that the hotel accommodation is directly linked to the destination in many ways. The decline or the development of a destination impacts the success of the hotel.

A changing location does not continually have negative effects on a property. For example, much of Tsim Sha Tsui in Hong Kong is built on reclaimed land on the Kowloon side of Hong Kong harbor. The Shangri-La Kowloon was built there in the early 1980s. At that time it was considered to be a luxury location, but by 2004 the area had deteriorated significantly.

Has the hotel's location changed much over the years?

Tsim Sha Tsui peaked in the 80s, then from middle of 90s we were a little overshadowed by Hong Kong side where a lot of hotels were built with convention centers and displays. Hong Kong island has been enjoying good feng shui for the last decade or so. Everything that goes up will come down so Tsim Sha Tsui will enjoy the glory very soon. There have been a lot of road works in this area for some time. That is why a lot of shops moved out because the walking traffic was less than before, apart from the hotels, restaurants, discos, and nightclubs. Now with the Kowloon Canton railway (underground) extension, people can take the train to go to the border of China easily. The actual station is just at the doorstep of this hotel. We feel this is very positive for this hotel.

(Belinda Goh, Director, Sales & Marketing,
Shangri-La Kowloon, Hong Kong)

This demonstrates one example of how location can change. Since the new underground is located as an extension to the major connecting point to China through Hung Hom station, the hotel's purpose location is now different. In addition, since the return of Hong Kong to China in July 1997 there has been a growing demand for accommodations by Chinese business people. The interview continued:

In what other ways have the changes in China affected your hotel?

There has been a relaxation of government controls in Quanxho. China is opening her doors in and out—that advantages Hong Kong. China has become quite an influential market for Hong Kong in general especially for retail and the tourist. Of course we are seeing the potential in the China market and it has grown for this hotel from single digits to slightly over 10 percent, standing about 12 percent at the moment—the market from China has potential for growth.

(Patsy Chan, Director, Communications,
Shangri-La Kowloon, Hong Kong)

As has been indicated, environmental scanning needs to be a constant process. A changing environment has serious implications for the management of a hotel.

What external factors have affected your hotel occupancy?

An example is that we do not have our own golf course like many hotels in the region. We are surrounded by twenty-five golf courses and that attracts a lot of British guests. The number of golf courses is a very good draw. But an interesting problem about local golf courses is that they have increased green fees so high that it adds too much to the cost and has therefore reduced attractiveness for the British market. As a result they now play golf in England, or France.

(Toni Alvarez, Director,
Hotel Beatriz Palace, Fuengirola, Spain)

Changes beyond the control of the hotel, such as the increase of green fees, directly impact occupancy. Changes in traffic flows, movement of business head offices, changes to flight schedules, introduction of new transport systems and schedules may not be significant in themselves individually but an accumulation of a variety of factors can have a significant impact.

LOCATION AND NEW PROPERTY DEVELOPMENT

Developing a new hotel and deciding on the number of rooms it should have, as suggested by Culligan (1990, p. 32) is a function of three factors. These are (1) the existing base of competitive hotels, (2) additions to the competitive hotel supply, and (3) deletions or effective removal of rooms from the competitive supply. Investing in the construction of a hotel property has a large number of risks. As reported by Brian (2003, p. 23) these include location, property type, asset performance, and sponsorship.

Often international hotel chains gain access to hotel markets through the development of Greenfield sites, acquisition of existing hotels, acquiring stakes in new and existing hotels, and management contracting and franchising; all of which are capital investment decisions (Tse & West, 1992; Collier & Gregory, 1995). These decisions are taken and implemented within a social organizational context by decision makers who have different perceptions and interpretations of what is necessary concerning the importance of location (Northcott, 1992). Development directors are key decision makers; they contribute to the expansion of international hotel groups through developing and implementing the development strategy within a designated geographic location. As such, the introduction of a hotel brand into a location can change that location by bringing new business through brand recognition, as well as impacting current properties both positively and negatively. For example, regarding urban tourism, it is suggested that the primary factor in its development is the accommodations (Arbel & Pizam, 1977). Without the hotel facility for the tourist to stay in, even the most richly attractive city could not become a major tourist destination.

Experience indicates that often insignificant research is carried out into the demand of additional accommodation rooms in an area before investors make a decision to develop a new property. Probably the best example is that of Singapore in the early 1980s. During this time, Singapore was an emerging tourism destination (Astbury, 1985, 1986; Smith, 1986). A number of hotel developers saw it as a place where there would be further growth in tourism and therefore a suitable place for investment in the development of additional hotel room stock. The unfortunate thing was that the various developers did not consult between themselves as to what impact the addition of more hotel rooms within the market may have. Over a short period of time a very large number of hotel rooms were added to the market; the oversupply resulted in very low room rates and because of this, hotels being converted into hospitals, offices, and other uses. Similar experiences have occurred in varying degrees around the world.

A problem such as this has occurred in Spain.

What impact has there been from hotel development in Spain?

So many new hotels have been opened in the last two or three years that the market has been literally flooded and this means that hotels are having to work harder to keep the same number of customers. Overall guests are paying less because the hotelier is trying not to lose their business. So it is not an easy situation.

(Rafael de la Fuente, Director Gerente, Escuela de Hosteleria, Benalmadena Pueblo, Spain)

The impact of new development is evident and follows a very predictable pattern. A new property entering the market has a number of different outcomes:

- Some guests staying at other properties move to the new property.
- To attract guests to the new hotel, initially the rates are set very competitively.
- Other properties respond by reducing their rate.
- New guests are attracted to the area. Room rates gradually increase.

Introducing additional new capacity into a market almost always results in a decline in overall room rates; the basic reason for this is that hotel management are not simply going to sit back and let competitors take their guests without any response. Alternatively, a much better approach could be to use the introduction to develop new market niches and expand the market overall (Hsu & Powers, 2002). It is suggested that there should be more emphasis placed on controlling supply growth, and more effort placed on the development of ways to encourage travel and growth in the hotel market (Higley, 2003).

LOCATION AND SOCIAL IMPACT

Often, the locations where developers wish to build hotels are as close as possible to the attraction that encourages the guest in the first place. These developments cannot be considered in isolation. Where a destination can be considered attractive to tourists and therefore a likely site for hotel development, the building of the hotel can change that environment.

What impact has the hotel development had on the landscape and environment?

This is a very complicated situation. Perhaps it is too late to have discovered that the landscape projection codes have been enforced in a very lenient way. In some cases they didn't even exist. So the authorities are beginning to realize now there is a major problem on their hands. The rate the building is going on the landscape will undoubtedly suffer in the future if it is not suffering already. Also there is another problem with lack of water resources. This is a very dry area and we are having an exceptionally dry year. There are many apartments owned by people in the United Kingdom and Europe as holiday homes. If all the people who own an apartment decided to come at the same time there wouldn't be enough water for the hotels. The authorities are beginning to realize it is a much better idea to develop your infrastructure before the hotels arrive.

(Rafael de la Fuente, Director Gerente,
Escuela de Hosteleria, Benalmedena Pueblo, Spain)

Hotels are heavy users of resources and heavy polluters. The impacts caused by the development of a hotel have been demonstrated in many research projects. A similar example was a hotel built in an attractive coastal region where the hotel guests used large quantities of water in comparison to the local residents. The water table changed, which allowed seawater to enter the water supply, causing it to become salty, thereby affecting the water supply for the whole community. There is now a growing interest in "green" hotels to reduce the impact hotels have on society and the environment, although much of the push is simply an attempt to reduce costs (Conner, 2000; Chan & Lam, 2001; Jim, 2000; Cukier, 2002).

LOCATION AND EMPLOYMENT OPPORTUNITIES

Hotels employ a lot of people—in many places internationally there are two or more employees for every guest in the hotel. The location of a hotel in a particular destination can provide potential employment opportunities that can be positive.

On the other hand, it could also be detrimental to the location because of such issues as prostitution, crime, relocation of the population, overcrowding of employees' living areas, and so on. Examples of the "pull" that hotels have on a population can be seen in many parts of the world, for example, in Hawaii, where once much of the food was locally grown on farms with a thriving farming community. Today, however, many of these people have moved to the main tourist areas in Honolulu, leaving their traditional lifestyles behind, attracted by what was perceived as a good financial return.

You are located quite a long way from the populated areas of the is-land—how does that impact staff availability?

That is a huge issue for us at Turtle bay, being so far away from the city where the majority of the population is. We have a very limited labor pool. When this hotel opened thirty years ago the majority of the staff came from the sugar cane fields because there were sugar refineries and mills and they were shutting down because that industry was going out of business. A lot of that crew was retrained and started working in this hotel. Some of the staff have been with us for years, but it is very hard to find new people in this part of the island.

(Abid Butt, Managing Director,
Turtle Bay Resort, Hawaii)

In addition, the development of high-rise hotels in city areas has brought about its own problems both for the local population and the tourist, such as greater traffic congestion and increased pollution. In many instances the burden for improving and dealing with these issues falls on the local tax paying community.

Alternatively, hotel development in specific areas can also result in labor shortages, which could push up costs and the availability of appropriately skilled staff.

This village is small and somewhat isolated—what impact does this have upon staffing?

Property prices up here are just ridiculous, also rental accommodation doesn't come up very often and if it does, it is very expensive. The living accommodation problem is difficult for us. We have managed to procure a house recently where we have four staff living. However, as we are getting busier we need to bring more people in but we have nowhere to put them. The other option is to pay them more money and say you have to find something yourself. When we bring staff in, they must have somewhere to live—they want a whole package and this difficult to do.

(Simon Rogan, Manager,
L'enclume, Cartmel, Cumbria, England)

For further reading, turn to the chapter on human resources where there are examples of how hotels in Shenzhen, China and Dallas are dealing with these issues.

SUMMARY

This chapter has discussed a number of major issues involved in the location of a hotel property. Although a management team may feel that there is little they can do about the location of their property, they do need to bear in mind how the location impacts issues such as room rate, the community, and attractiveness of the property and how these are perceived by the guest. A continual environmental-scanning approach should always be operating to take into account the changes that are taking place in the location and how those changes are impacting the hotel. The location selected for the building of a hotel not only has internal impacts, but also affects its surrounding neighborhood and because of this, hotel management in many areas has become directly involved in community affairs, such as voluntary groups, local political groups, and other community based organizations, thus ensuring the community identity of the establishment, allowing it a "voice" in local affairs and making certain the hotel has a friendly community "face."

DISCUSSION

A. As the manager of a hotel just about to open in a location with many competitors, how could you operate without negatively influencing the market's local room rate?

B. What are some of the negative issues that the location selected for a new hotel can have on a community?

C. What issues do you see as the most important when selecting a location for a new hotel development?

D. What issues would you consider when undertaking environmental scanning?

E. As a manager of a hotel in your local area, what community groups would you be involved with?

F. Think about two or three different locations for a hotel and analyze how the local staff can help you understand the issues faced by them.

G. Is there an opportunity for hotel managers of different hotels in the same location (i.e., competitors) to cooperate together on some issues? If so, what should these be?

H. You have been appointed as a manager of a first class hotel located in an isolated area—what management decisions do you make?

CASE STUDIES

Case 1.1. Turtle Bay Resort, Hawaii

The Turtle Bay Resort is located on the windward side of the island of Oahu, the most visited by international guests of any of the Hawaiian Islands. The main area where visitors stay is in Waikiki, which is situated just a few miles from the international airport. In comparison the Turtle Bay Resort is almost as far away from the airport and Waikiki as is possible. Since the 1960s Waikiki has developed as a major tourism destination. This has resulted in a large number of hotels being built in a fairly small geographical area. In many respects Waikiki caters now for the mass market. Viewing Web sites such as http://www.hawaii-hotel.com/ gives an indication of the large number of hotels and the price competition among those hotels. This competition has resulted in high levels of discounting and a commodification of the market. For many years Waikiki has worked under a "price war" environment just to keep the rooms full. "They are not able to raise the rates because the people do not appreciate any price increase, and as a result the rate slides in a very small range, which is less that Maui or Hawaii could charge. Waikiki is now like anywhere United States—it does not give you a feeling of a resort."

The Turtle Bay Resort is quite different from that. Although there is a problem with it being a long distance from the Airport and Waikiki, its location also gives it significant advantages. It is clearly in a different market, and therefore does not have to compete on price. The location also allows for golf courses and other outdoor facilities in a park resort environment which is not available in Waikiki.

Abid Butt, Managing Director, Turtle Bay Resort

Questions

1. If you were the manager of the Turtle Bay Resort how could you further use the location to your benefit?
2. How could you as a manager benefit from the long travel time from the airport to the hotel?
3. As manager of the hotel what association would you have with the hotels in Waikiki?

Case 1.2. Hotel Locations in the Chinese Cities

Abstract

*This case reports on empirical research in three Chinese cities to test the Egan and Nield (2002) model of hotel location. The authors conclude that the Egan and Nield model is applicable to Chinese cities and that a hierarchy of hotels related to spatial location is observable. However, the complexity of Chinese cities and the current rapid expansion that is changing the spatial structure of the planned Chinese cities mean that, whilst the model can predict the general spatial pattern of hotel location, refinement is required in order to take account of agglomerative tendencies identified in the location of hotels in Chinese Cities.

Introduction

This paper presents some initial analysis of a study of hotel location in three Chinese cities. The work is part of a larger study that aims to develop an optimizing model to help identify how important location is in the success of new and existing hotels. In this paper the authors report the successful application of an urban location model initially developed in the United Kingdom. The successful predictions of the model in both the U.K. and Chinese markets suggest that the model is identifying common principles underlying the location choice of hotels.

The question of location is fundamental to the success of a hotel. Ellsworth Sattler, founder of the Sattler hotel chain and one of the pioneers of marketing in the hospitality industry, once said there were three factors necessary for the success of a hotel: location, location, and location (cited in Hsu & Powers, 2002). It can be argued that the hotel location is part of the product and service of the hotel itself, for it not only involves the convenience issue but also shapes the segmentation of the market. There is very limited literature on hotel location—Bull (1994), Pearce (1995), Ashworth and de Haan (1985), Roubi and Litteljohn (2004) as regards to the booming hotel sector in Chinese cities note that nothing significant appears to have been written regarding the location of Chinese hotels. The Chinese hotel industry provides an interesting case for the study of hotel location as the current boom in hotel developments in certain Chinese cities creates the opportunity to test the hotel location model developed by the authors.

A different approach to understanding hotel location has been developed by Roubi and Litteljohn (2004) who suggest that perhaps the often quoted notion of "location, location, and location" for hotel success could be expanded into: location (prosperity of the area), location (general access to

---

*Egan, D., Chen, W., and Zhang, Y. (n.d.). "The intra-urban location of hotels in the Chinese cities of Beijing, Shanghai & Shenzhen." Paper presented at CHME Conference, Bournemouth. Used with permission.

tourism business/commerce and travel infrastructure), and location (imme-diate proximity to facilities and positioning in the local environment). It has also been suggested that accessibility and transportation systems are in-creasingly important for urban development and hotel location by Kevin and Lam (2001), who note that it is generally recognized that the preferred choices for hotel locations are close to the airport, train station, bus inter-change, and highway interchange. Zoning can bring clusters of target cus-tomers to hotels and create new location choices for the hotel business.

Although there are some differences in these approaches, the reality is that the underlying principles are the same, the difference is largely in terms of the detail reflecting the starting point of the authors; the Roubi and Litteljohn (2004) work comes from a hospitality perspective whereas the Egan and Nield's work (2001) comes from an urban location theory perspec-tive. The Egan and Nield model has been applied to other hospitality set-tings with some success (Egan, Knowles, & Bey, 2000; Egan & Ball, 2004). By combining the two approaches it is possible that a better understanding of the optimum location requirements of hotels may be identifiable. The long-term aim of this research is to develop an optimizing model to predict the ideal location for different types of hotels. This particular study is a case study to test the general applicability of the model that is being developed by applying it to the dynamic market of urban China.

The Hotel Location Model

In our model of intra-urban hotel location we adopt the traditional neoclas-sical economic perspective that emphasizes the role of accessibility and rent in determining land use via a process of competitive bidding. The model is based on the partial-equilibrium bid-rent approach, developed by various economists in the late 1960s. The bid-rent model represents a development of the von Thünen (1826) model of agricultural land use, which was applied in an urban context by Isard (1956). This was further developed by Alonso (1964) into the concept of the bid-rent function, the approach to be employed to explain hotel location. It is important to note that Alonso's approach is concerned with partial equilibrium. By contrast, the New Urban Econom-ics, developed in the 1970s, is based on a general equilibrium approach (Richardson, 1977). It is our contention, however, that a partial approach, with all its limitations, can still be a useful tool for analyzing the behavior of activities such as hotels, which exhibit a spatial hierarchy of land use.

Alonso, in his original formulation for the slope of the bid-rent curve, presented the following equation:

$$dp/dt = (V_t - C_v \, V_t - C_t \,)/q$$

where dp is a change in the bid rent with respect to a change in distance; dt is the change in location; V_t is marginal revenue lost from moving an additional unit of distance t away from the center; C_vV_t is marginal operating costs arising from the change in volume of business V_t (indirect effect of movement on operating costs); C_t is marginal increases in operating costs arising directly from a change in t and q is the quantity of land.

Thus the change in bid price is equal to the change in volume of business minus the volume of business minus the change in operating costs. Alonso makes the assumptions that, first, the volume of business will decrease with increasing distance from the city center, so that V_t is negative; second, operating costs will rise so that the change will be positive, but preceded by a minus sign, and third, the quantity of land must be positive, the slope of the bid-rent curve must be negative. Alonso (1964, p. 55) notes that the slope will be such that the savings in land costs are just equal to the business lost plus the increase in operating costs. Thus the family of bid-rent curves is very like an indifference map—the curves, being single-valued, do not cross and slope to the right.

In the model the change in bid-rent is equal to the change in revenue minus the change in non-land costs, divided by the size of the site. Equilibrium is achieved by maximizing profits, the lowest attainable bid-rent indicating the highest-level profits, because land costs are minimized. In effect, hotels are trading off the benefit of a location against the costs, the presumption being that a hotel is looking for an optimal location that is, a location which maximizes profits.

The obvious question from the viewpoint of a non-urban economist is, why one would expect a spatial hierarchy of hotels within urban areas? To understand the process we feel it is important to go back to the foundations of urban economics and in particular the nature of the urban land market. The history of urban development in China is different from the Western world where the Alonso model was developed, therefore a discussion and review of the underlying principles and their potential applicability, and hence the suitability of the model is critical to analyze the Chinese Hotel market.

A useful starting point is to consider what is often referred to as the particular nature of urban land. Kivell (1993) notes that land is unlike most other commodities involved in the production process because it "possesses a number of unusual and complex characteristics." He suggests the following as being of particular importance: fixed supply in the sense that physical quantity of land is fixed; no cost of supply (land is often referred to as a free gift of nature); unique/irreplaceable; immobile; permanence. Most models of urban land use tend to assume that demand factors are more important than supply, for the reasons stated above, the usual assumption being that supply is inelastic and therefore it is demand that sets the price and therefore urban land use reflects the demand for a particular plot.

In a market economy it is usually assumed that land is allocated to the highest and best via the price mechanism.

Harvey (1987) suggests that theories involving market-based models of urban land use have assumptions, such as resources are allocated on the basis of prices, costs and profits; firms and households will have location preferences which are reflected in land prices and rents; owners sell and rent to the highest bidder; and there is no government interference.

Harvey (1987) also notes that, from the viewpoint of the individual firm, a number of general factors can be identified. The first factor is general accessibility to the center or CBD. This is traditionally viewed as the most accessible point and the focus for transport, labor, and retail markets, but with changes in transport systems this could be regarded as a somewhat heroic assumption. However, while there are serious doubts in many cities whether the CBD can be regarded as the most accessible point for transport, labor, and retail markets, we would suggest that, from the viewpoint of some parts of the hotel market, this would still appear to be the case. The second factor is special accessibility—usually associated with agglomeration economies, complementarities of businesses can be of particular relevance, and there are additional factors such as historical, topographical, and other special site characteristics.

Thus the demand for a site reflects an inseparable package of attributes, such as location, infrastructure, complementary activities, and transport; however this view only reflects the so-called user demand, those who actually wish to use the land. There is another group, investors, who hope to enjoy either flow of income from the users of the land and/or an increase in value from increases in demand in the future. It is the combination of these two groups which forms the actual market demand for urban land. Through the market, land will be allocated to the highest bidder. Thus the value of the land reflects the competitive bidding. Hotels are thus in competition with other users for land—the more desirable a location the higher the potential value.

From the viewpoint of an individual hotel the bidding will reflect their expected revenues and costs discounted to net present value which will in turn be reflected in their maximum bids. The behavior of a hotel may well vary. If it is viewed purely as a user, that is, the management is renting the site, only user value is of concern; however if a hotel site is also owned by the management, an additional factor is the possibility of capital growth in the future. This factor may be of greater importance in more speculative development such as urban regeneration where the future market may be much greater than the current position.

Although the above principles will apply to Chinese cities, particularly in the current market-led economy, it is useful to describe the urban development of Chinese cities. It is important to appreciate that in Chinese cities the role of government in the past has been significant in the location of hotels; in all economies the state has a major influence on land use. However market forces also have a major influence, particularly in the changing Chinese economy. The empirical research reported here is a review of the situation in 2004, and thus the picture presented reflects historical land use decisions and more recent market-led changes.

Urban Development and Land Use in Chinese Cities

Land-Use Reform in China

In China, from the 1960s to the 1970s, the economy was a planned econ-omy; there was a planned allocation of resources, so markets for factors of production did not exist. Factors of production, including land, raw materials, and machinery, were allocated by government. It has left many historical problems to the later development. Urban land use reform began in 1979 when the Chinese law on "Cooperative Ventures" allowed indigenous enter-prises to use their land as capital to cooperate with foreign investors (Ling & Isaac, 1994). Even with more recent land reform in China, the land use and land market is unusual in that it is still affected by the historical factors to a large degree. Chen and Wills (1999) argue that one of the most efficient ways of allocating land to different users is to allow bid-rent allocation to take place. This will lead to users choosing their optimum location and therefore maximizing economic efficiency. In this way rent depends on the actual de-mand and supply for different uses. When land occupation does not involve a monetary cost, the result is that competition for land use depends mainly on the priority given by the State administration to various enterprises (China). This special phenomena can explain why the number of high-end hotels is so large, but their room-rate is not economically viable in China. One of the reasons is that the land use did not take into account the invest-ment cost in most state-owned hotels.

Another historical factor that had a major influence on the development of Chinese Cities before economic reform was the emphasis on the growth of heavy industries. This policy has left a huge supply of old factory buildings in the city center area. Moreover, it has created redevelopment opportunities for hotel developments. Recent research by Zhu (2003) on land develop-ment in Shanghai found that quite a number of manufacturing factories occupied central locations in downtown Shanghai. Zhu argued that this is a legacy of the pre-reform era of socialist industrialization when urban land was a free means of production and industrialist demand overtook that of others in land allocation, it was not unusual to see factories located in the central business district and now redevelopment of the old central city was hampered by the existing land use. In 1985, 56.7 percent of all factories in Shanghai municipality were in its central city, where it was estimated that 30 percent of the land area was occupied by factories and warehouses (Fung et al., 1992). This arguably inappropriate factory location in a Chinese city has provided a special opportunity to the hotel business, especially the bud-get hotel. In fact, the opportunity lies behind the current boom in downtown budget hotels by hotel investors in China, such as the most famous domestic budget hotel chain: Jinjiang Star. One of the location strategies of Jinjiang Star is to demolish old factory buildings and rebuild budget hotels on the sites. Furthermore, redeveloping the old factory buildings is an effi-cient option for investors. If the land was previously allocated by the state, developers just need to pay enough money for demolition and rehabilitation and a nominal premium to get the land, so the prospective users can make a huge profit (Ling & Isaac, 1994). This phenomena lies behind the opinion of many in the Chinese hotel industry that the domestic hotel company has advantages over the international hotel company to develop the budget hotel business because of these land supply issues.

Structure Change of Land Use in Metropolitan China

We suggest that the Chinese metropolitan evolution theory of Song (2003) is a good explanation of an observed pattern of hotel location as described later in this book. Song (2003) argued that there were have three phases of the structure change of land use in metropolitans in China. The first phase was the "industrialization suburban" where the old heavy industries located in the city center moved out to the suburban area as they were under the pressure of transport, environment, and land price factors. The second phase was the "resident and service industry suburban" that indicated there was multifunctional communities around the urban fringe area. The third phase was the "urban extending" that indicated the "secondary industrialization suburban." The cities of Beijing or Shanghai showed the same pattern of the structure change of land use during urban development. The hotel location pattern also changed along with it. In terms of the key trends, the pattern, as described by Song (2003), is not dissimilar to the pattern of change to be found in European and American cities (Kivell, 1993). If we now consider the land use and hotel location of the three case study cities.

The City of Beijing

The structure of land use changed in the city of Beijing during three phases. The first phase formed the "urban-rural dichotomy pattern." In the 1950s, the Beijing government focused on the heavy industry development that underlay the population boom and the city center conglomeration. During the first development phase the core of the old city was formed, comprising four districts: Dongcheng, Xicheng, Congwen, and Xuanwu.

The second phase formed the "urban-rural ternary pattern." In the 1980s, with economic reform, the urban and rural cross-pervasion began, especially after the land reform that regulated the competition of land use which resulted in heavy industry moving out of the city center to the suburban area. At the same time, the high-value service industries (finance, insurance, offices, media, etc.) continuously congregated in the city center where was formed the Guomao CBD, Yansha CBD, and two financial streets in Beijing. During this phase, the high-end hotels congregated in the CBD area or other center areas. At the same time, the lower quality hotels also positioned themselves in vantage points around the center area. During the "resident suburban" period, there appeared huge growth of the resident area around the fringe of the city that continuously occupied the industry land. Hence, the heavy industry moved further out of the suburban area to the Economy and Technology Development Zone, creating new supply opportunities to hotel investors.

The third phase formed the "urban-rural integration pattern." Suburban and rural areas became more and more integrative, along with the further development of Zhongguancun High Technology Park, the Olympic Park, the Capital airport, trolley, highway network, and so on, the changing structure of land use causing changes to the hotel location pattern in the city. For example, several quality hotels located at the edge of the city were built, the common characteristic being their location near the main road, thus providing easy access for guests to both the city center and airport (usually ten-fifteen minutes driving).

The City of Shanghai

The structure of land use change in the city of Shanghai is similar to that of Beijing. In the 1990s Shanghai set out proposals to become an international metropolitan city. The new urban plan required the structure of land use in Shanghai to adapt to reflect its development as an international economic center, international financial center, international trade center, international ship center, and so on. Hence, the heavy industry was forced to move out of the city center, to be replaced by the finance, stock, trade, and management industries. However, the second phase in land use change in Shanghai is different to that of Beijing. For reasons of geography Beijing has developed not via the "circle pattern" to extend its urban land, but rather the "agglomeration pattern" to extend the urban area. Most notable being the Pudong New Area resulting in the creation of the Lujiazui Financial Centre, Jinqiao Export Processing Zone, Waigaoqiao Tariff Free Zone, Zhangjiang High Technology Park in Pudong district. Now the CBD of Shanghai includes the Bund area, North Bund area, and Xiao Lujiazui area (total 5 sq km.) where the majority of banks, international group headquarters, and other high-class service industries are located. The CCD (Centre Commercial District) includes the area north from the Changshou road and south to the Fuxing road; west from the Wulumuqi road and east to the whole Da Lujiazui area (total 30 sq km.), where the density of buildings is very high and the opportunities for redevelopment is significant. Interestingly, from our research we discovered that most hotels built in the past five years are concentrated in the New Pudong area and the old city center. One reason could be the supply factors, where the old city center provided many redevelopment opportunities suited to hotel developments.

The City of Shenzhen

Separated only by a river from Hong Kong, Shenzhen used to be a small frontier town with a population of less than 30,000. The Central Government established the Shenzhen Special Economic Zone (SSEZ) in 1980 as one of the four testing grounds for the importation of foreign capital and integration with the world economy. With rapid growth and modernization during the past two decades, Shenzhen grew to a population of 7 million—a city of immigrants. The region, which covers about 2,000 sq km., has changed from a farming region to a highly urbanized area with a built-up area of 470 sq km. Shenzhen's current output per capita is among the highest in China.

The SSEZ, with a total area of 327.5 sq km., was built on a greenfield site with a few small towns, the most important of which was Luohu and the main customs checkpoint on the border between the mainland of China and Hong Kong. At the very early stage of development, the general target was "to develop Shenzhen into industry-led modernized Special Economic Zones, based on the integration of agricultural and industrial development" (Gu, 1998). Urban development was mainly in industrial zones. According to the first Comprehensive Plan, made in 1982, Shenzhen would be developed into a linear city stretching along the border between Shenzhen and Hong Kong.

In the "Shenzhen Comprehensive Plan" (1996-2010), the planned area was extended beyond the SSEZ to cover the entire metropolitan region. It aimed to build Shenzhen into a major city that offered finance, commerce, trade, information technology, transportation services, and high technology. Shenzhen was expected to be a prosperous and well-managed city that was attractive to tourists and a comfortable place to live (Wang et al., 2000).

During this phase, using Hong Kong as a reference, Shenzhen began to draft the Urban Planning Ordinances in 1995, when a new planning system was brought forward. The Regulatory Planning & Ordinance was then regarded as the key connection between urban planning theory and its practice (Xue & Zhou, 1999). The Ordinance took effect in 1998 and led urban planning in Shenzhen. A new Urban Planning Board was also established according to the Ordinance. In 1999, the first eleven "regulatory plans and ordinances" were put into effect in accordance with the statutory procedure.

Tourism Impact on Urban Development in China

China is currently one of the most dynamic tourist economies in the world and its tourism facilities and services are rapidly improving. Tourism is now viewed as a means of attracting foreign exchange, providing employment, promoting regional development, and stimulating economic growth. The tourism industry is now regarded as one of the main stimuli of urban development in China.

Tourism Policy and Urban Development

Chinese tourism policies have established a legal framework for the administration, management, and operation of tourism enterprises. This framework has covered almost all aspects of the tourism industry (Zhang, King, & Jenkins, 2002). The China National Tourism Administration, functioning under the State Council, is the administrative organ of the nation's tourism trade. One of its functions is to formulate policies and establish systems for developing tourism. It has branches in all provinces, autonomous regions, and municipalities. The most significant benefit brought to the urban evolution by tourism policy is the development of infrastructure.

About twenty-five years ago, the third generation chairman and the chief designer of Chinese reform and opening, Deng Xiaoping, said: the government should pay a great attention to both tourism and urban development; developing tourism should consider the city's infrastructures improving at the same time (CNTA, 2000a). Under the golden rule of Deng Xiaoping, Chinese government in each province has invested a large sum of capital on infrastructure building in order to attract more foreign and domestic travelers, especially in the coastal cities, as these have more "higher quality travelers" than inland cities. In 2000, the Chinese government launched the tourism infrastructure building into "national debt planning," 1.3 billion RMB was invested in infrastructure building, the main focus being on tourism transport, water and electricity provision, car parking, public toilets, sewerage and garbage disposal (CNTA, 2000b). In 2001, the Shanghai government pointed out that in order to develop and optimize urban tourism resources in the city of Shanghai, all tourism transport should be greatly improved. All airport, railway, highway, and water carriage transport should be based on the principle of bringing convenience to tourists. The tourism planning of new Shanghai focuses on improving urban sightseeing, business conferences, shopping, and other far-suburb nature tourism (Shanghai Guildhall, 2001). The Guangdong government made out a new tourism policy in 2002 in order to keep in step with the reform and development of the tourism industry, the government should support the building of infrastructure, transport, the special tourism line, car parking, bus stops, and the green belt around the landscape and hotels (Guangdong Guildhall, 2002). All these positive tourism policies in China not only created a pleasant tourism environment but also stimulated the evolution of urban areas throughout the country. At the same time, we can see the hotel location pattern changed with this urban evolution in China.

In the Alonso model, the problem is conceived in terms of the location decision of the individual household or firm which is facing a given rent-distance function. Such a rent gradient is exogenous to the model, a major shortcoming in the explanation of urban form. However, from the viewpoint of a particular firm (i.e., a hotel) this reflects the context of the decision-making process. The Alonso model is based on the assumption of a mono-centric city, which lies on a featureless plain, and from which transport is possible in every direction. All urban employment exists at the city center and all foodstuffs and services are only available at that location, the land market being competitive and free from institutional constraints and other distortions. These assumptions allow residential location, the main concern of the Alonso model, to be analyzed in one-dimensional space in terms of the cost of commuting from residence to the city center. The bid-rent concept is, however, applicable to non-residential establishments such as hotels.

Alonso makes the following assumptions: the volume of business will decrease with increasing distance from the city center, so that V_t is negative;

operating costs will rise, so that the change will be positive, but preceded by a minus sign; the quantity of land must be positive. Thus the slope of the bid-rent curve must be negative. Alonso (1964, p. 55) notes that the slope will be such that the savings in land costs are just equal to the business lost plus the increase in operating costs. Thus the family of bid-rent curves is very like an indifference map, the curves being single-valued, nonintersecting, and downward sloping to the right.

This model can be used to explain hotel location, although the significance of the individual components is rather different from that perceived by Alonso. In the case of hotels, the value of the product can be expected to vary with distance from the center, our proposition being that there is an inverse relationship between revenue and distance from the city center, whereas Alonso regarded the relationship between costs and distance as particularly significant. In the case of hotels, costs are unlikely to vary with location to any significant extent, so that in our view C_t is unlikely to change significantly with distance from the city center, while in the case of hotels, V_t, will vary significantly with distance from the city center.

In the model, the change in bid-rent is equal to the change in revenue minus the change in nonland costs, divided by the size of the site. Equilibrium is achieved by maximizing profits, the lowest attainable bid-rent indicating the highest-level profits, since land costs are minimized. In effect, hotels are trading off the benefit of a location against the costs, the presumption being that a hotel is looking for an optimal location—that is, a location that maximizes profits.

Underlying this analysis are the assumptions that firms benefit from centrality and that revenues fall and costs increase toward the edge of the city center. These assumptions underlie the bid-rent curves and the land-value or rent gradient (curve SS). This indicates the relationship between land costs and location. In effect, curve SS indicates the profile of expected land costs facing a business looking to bid for a location. The rent gradient has long been regarded as a serious weakness of the Alonso model. Richardson (1977) notes that the rent gradient is assumed and not therefore, endogenous to the model. The rent gradient can be made endogenous, however, if the bid-rent functions of all activities are known and if it is possible to fix a priori one point on the rent gradient itself, such as the rent at the city center or the rent of marginal land at the city boundary, this being derived from agricultural land prices. If these two conditions are satisfied, the rent gradient may be constructed from overlapping bid-rent functions, ranked by their steepness and position with respect to the city center. Such a rent gradient can be linked to the Burgess (1925) model of concentric zones of land use.

Each of the family of bid-rent curves (brc) is similar to an indifference map in that it shows all the possible relationships between land costs and those revenues and costs that vary with location. A bid-rent curve can be viewed as a visual representation of the potential trade-off facing a business between productivity of a location (as determined by distance from the city center) and land costs, which are also determined by distance from the city center and are shown by the curve SS, as defined above. The shape of the bid-rent curve for an individual business will be determined by the relationship between the net productivity of locations (defined as the difference between revenue and nonland costs). Those activities that have steep bid-rent curves will outbid those activities with flatter curves, reflecting the relative productivities of locations with distance from the city center. The preference will be for the lowest attainable bid-rent curve, since this will have the lowest land costs and, under the assumption of profit maximization, will therefore be the optimal location. The lowest attainable bid-rent curve will be the one that is tangential to the SS curve.

The problem is, of course, that bid-rent analysis is based on a tautology. Although this can be the subject of theoretical debate, we have chosen to adopt a more pragmatic approach and to view the curve SS as an indicator of the actual land-value gradient. Obviously, the actual shape of the gradient will vary from city to city depending, as noted above, on a range of socioeconomic factors operating in a historical context. However, because the shape of the land-value gradient will influence the shape of the bid-rent curve by influencing (via land costs) the costs at different locations, the tautological nature of the bid-rent curve can be viewed as a strength for our purposes, partly because it reflects the reality in which hotel operators have to weigh up the costs of a location against potential revenues, and partly because it suggests that the bid-rent concept is also dynamic and that its evolution reflects changing urban patterns. In the case of urban hotels, it seems likely that revenues will tend to fall with distance from the center, although this represents something of a simplification. If we assume that non-land costs are constant over space, then potential revenues should determine the maximum potential bids for land within the urban area. Working from these assumptions, the optimal location for different hotel sectors can be predicted.

Empirical Analysis

Underlying the above analysis are the assumptions that firms benefit from centrality and that revenues fall and costs increase with movement to locations at the edge of the city center. This is the essential proposition we are testing in this particular case study.

The initial analysis of the empirical data, while supporting the predictions of the model, has identified a number of issues which suggest that the model could be developed further to take account of complexities of these Chinese cities, reflecting their rapid recent growth (Chen and Wills, 1999; Ling and Isaac, 1994; Song and Zhang, 2002; Song, 2003; Zhu, 2003).

The empirical research reported here involved the plotting of the spatial location of a sample of urban hotels and an analysis of room prices by location.

However, due to the sheer size of these cities it was impossible to survey the whole cities, so selected spatial areas were identified, these areas are summarized in Exhibit 1.1. The methodology used was based on gathering data from the Internet by looking at the Web sites of individual hotels, the information was then initially plotted on a map of the appropriate city so a picture of hotel location could be identified. The areas surveyed are shown

EXHIBIT 1.1. Analysis of Spatial Areas

The Scale of Hotels	Total Number of Hotels Identified in Each Area			Number in Sample		
	Shanghai	Beijing	Shenzhen	Shanghai	Beijing	Shenzhen
5-star hotel	20	32	10	20 (100%)	30 (94%)	9 (90%)
4-star hotel	30	65	19	30 (100%)	32 (50%)	10 (50%)
3-star hotel	124	197	69	50 (40%)	50 (25%)	15 (30%)
Total	174	294	98	100 (58%)	112 (38%)	34 (35%)

Areas Surveyed in the City of Beijing, Shanghai, and Shenzhen

Name of Area	Name of City		
	Beijing	Shanghai	Shenzhen
CCD (Centre Commercial District)	WangFuJing Street	NanJing Road	DongMen Road
Old CBD (Centre Business District)	Guomao CBD	JingAn, HuangPu CBD	RenMingNan CBD

	Yansha CBD	LuJiaZui CBD	HuaQiangBei CBD
New CBD or Finance CBD	Yansha CBD	LuJiaZui CBD	HuaQiangBei CBD
Transition Zone (Between old CBD and new CBD)	Worker's Stadium	Naught	Transition Zone
International Conference & Exhibition Centre	China International Exhibition Centre	International Conference Centre	CHTF Exhibition Centre
High Technology Zone	ZhongGuanCun	HongQiao	NanShan
Intra-Urban Tourism Area	QianMen	The Bund	HuaQiaoCheng
Airport Area	Capital Airport	HongQiao Airport	BaoAn Airport
Railway Station, Bus Interchange, Highway Interchange	West Railway Station	Shanghai Railway Station	Luohu Railway Station
University Area	HaiDian District	Yangpu District	Naught
Sports Centre	Worker's Stadium & FengTai Sports Centre	Hongkou Stadium & Shanghai Stadium	Shenzhen Stadium

in Exhibit 1.1. The types of hotel in each of the spatial areas were then identified, then the pattern of room rates were plotted against the different zones.

Exhibit 1.2 presents a summary of the results of the location survey. The cities were initially categorized by different zones to reflect the theoretical accessibility and potential agglomeration economies as identified by Egan and Nield (2001). An analysis of hotel types by location zones broadly fits with the predictions of the Egan and Nield model, however the existence of two CBDs requires further work on the Egan and Nield model. The results also suggest that the agglomeration economies may be of more importance in Chinese cities or alternatively the sheer size of these cities means that the zones should be considered in a different way for the purposes of modeling. Exhibit 1.2 clearly shows a hierarchy of hotel types by spatial location as predicted by the Egan and Nield model; however, as already noted, because of the complexity of Chinese cities, a simple distance determination,

EXHIBIT 1.2. Results of Location Survey

Hotel Location and Site	Hotel Category		
	5- and 4-Star Hotels	3-Star Hotel	Budget Hotel
CCD (*Centre Commercial District*)	3		
CBD (*Centre Business District*)	3		
Centre Finance Street	3		
Transition Zone (*Between old CBD and new CBD*)	3	3	
International Conference & Exhibition Centre	3	3	
High Technology Zone	3	3	
Intra-Urban Tourism Area	3	3	3
Airport Area		3	
Railway Station, Bus Interchange, Highway Interchange		3	3
University Area			3

while providing an adequate explanation of broad spatial patterns, is inadequate to fully explain the detailed spatial pattern. The results summarized in Exhibit 1.2 suggest that the existence of dual CBD creates an overlapping hierarchy of spatial location, plus the transition zone appears to be an area of overlap—further research is required here to identify whether an observable pattern within the zone of transition can be identified on the ground.

Exhibit 1.3, which presents data on room rates and location zones within Beijing, again reflects the expectations from the predictions of the Egan and Nield (2000) model regarding price: more central locations are preferred by most guests and this will be reflected in room prices. Indeed, the room rates reflect a centrality preference backed up with a willingness to pay within all the different hotel types. From the Beijing hotel location map (Figure 1.1), it

EXHIBIT 1.3. Room Rates and Location Zones

Hotel Site	Hotel Room-Rate and Category			
	5-Star Hotel (RMB)	4-Star Hotel (RMB)	3-Star Hotel (RMB)	Budget Hotel (RMB)
CCD (*Wang Fu Jing Commercial Street*)	2641.5	1535	702.7	
Old CBD (*Guomao CBD*)	2360.5	1447		
New CBD (*Yansha CBD*)	2134.2	1463.5	752	288
International Conference & Exhibition Centre		1333	588	
High Technology Zone (*Zhong Guan Cun*)	1770.2	1200	565	
Intra-Urban Tourism Area (*Qianmen, Tiantan Area*)			518	188
Intra-Urban Railway Station	1564	1182.9	492	178
University Area (*Haiding District*)				178
Sports Centre			533.3	178
Airport Area			558.8	

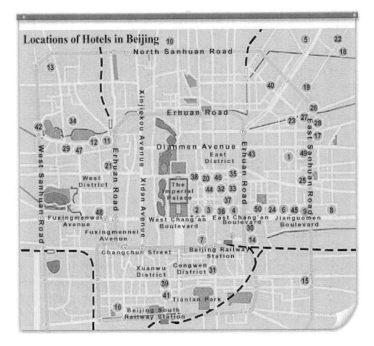

FIGURE 1.1. Locations of Hotels in Beijing

Map No	Hotel Name	Map No	Hotel Name
1	Beijing Asia Jinjiang Hotel	12	Exhibition Centre Hotel
2	Beijing Grand Hotel	13	Friendship Hotel
3	Beijing Hotel	14	Gloria Plaza Hotel
4	Beijing International Hotel	15	Golden Era Hotel
5	Beijing Movenpick Hotel	16	Grand View Garden Hotel
6	Hotel Beijing-Toronto	17	The Great Wall Sheraton Hotel
7	Capital Hotel	18	Harbour Plaza Hotel
8	China Resources Hotel	19	Hilton Hotel
9	China World Hotel	20	Holiday Inn Crowne Plaza
10	Continental Grand Hotel	21	Holiday Inn Downtown
11	Debao Hotel	22	Holiday Inn Lido

Map No	Hotel Name	Map No	Hotel Name
23	Huadu Hotel	38	Prime Hotel Beijing
24	Jianguo Hotel	39	Qianmen Hotel
25	Jing Guang New World Hotel	40	Radisson Sas Hotel Beijing
26	Kempinski Hotel Beijing	41	Rainbow Hotel
27	Kunlun Hotel	42	Shangri-La Hotel
28	Landmark Towers	43	Swissotel Hong Kong Macau Center
29	New Century Hotel	44	Tianlun Dynasty Hotel
30	Hotel New Otani Chang Fu Gong	45	Traders Hotel
31	New World Courtyard Beijing	46	Wangfujing Grand Hotel
32	Novotel Beijing	47	Xiyuan Hotel
33	Ocean Hotel	48	Yanjing Hotel
34	Olympic Hotel	49	Zhao Long Hotel
35	Overseas Chinese Hotel	50	Beijing International Club Hotel
36	The Palace Hotel		
37	Peace Hotel		

can be clearly identified that main luxury 4-star and 5-star hotels are located on WangFuJing Street (Centre Commercial District); Guomao Area (Old Centre Business District); Yansha Area (New Finance CBD); and China International Exhibition Centre Area (Conference & Exhibition Centre), which basically match Egan and Nield's (2001) model. The authors also realize that, as China has been going through the economic transition stages from central planning to market economy, traditionally government interference played an important role in the land resource allocation, which means it did not follow the urban land use assumption (Harvey, 1987). It is no surprise, therefore, to find that there are some low priced state-owned hotels in city-center areas in Beijing and Shanghai. These hotels were used for government officials and operated with objectives other than profits. Without sufficient management skills, these hotels could not compete with international or domestic hotel chains and now they are declining or utilized for other purposes. In the newly developed cities, such as Shenzhen and new development areas in Beijing and Shanghai, bidding for land has become the popular allocation method in recent years, which will make future Chinese hotel development follow the hotel location model more closely (Egan & Nield, 2001; Kevin & Lam, 2001).

Conclusions

This paper reports the initial analysis of the application of an urban optimizing model to hotel location in three Chinese cities. Although further research is required, a number of conclusions can be drawn from the results presented in this chapter. First, a pattern of urban location can be identified with regards to the location of hotels by type within these three Chinese cities. In addition, an analysis by room rates and location shows a clear spatial pattern both between specific hotel types and within particular hotel types, for example, budget hotels. The two observed patterns reported here correspond to the predictions made by the Egan and Nield (2000) model of hotel location. Of particular note is that the model was developed from a body of urban economic theory in the Anglo-American tradition. It appears that the underlying principles apply to Chinese Cities with their very different socioeconomic/cultural traditions. It should be possible to model the optimum location for particular hotel types. It should also be possible to model how the changing socioeconomic environment, with regards to tourism, may influence the optimum location of hotels. The next stage in the research is to consider how the complexity of Chinese Cities can be modeled, in particular the existence of dual CBDs, and to further refine the model to study the impact of agglomeration economies and identify those criteria specific to different locations.

REFERENCES

Alonso, W. (1964). *Location and land use: Towards a general theory of land rent.* Cambridge, MA: Harvard University.

Arbel, A., & Pizam, A. (1977). Some determinants of urban hotel location: The tourists' inclination. *Journal of Travel Research, 15*(3), 15-21.

Ashworth, G.J., & de Haan, T.Z. (1985). *The Tourist Historic City: A model and initial application in Norwich, U.K.*, Gronigen: University of Gronigen.

Astbury, S. (1985). Survival of the fittest in Singapore hotel war/discos scene of feverish activity/a smart turnout/'Regulation is the biggest enemy.' *Asia Business, 21*(11), 22-27.

Astbury, S. (1986). Economic report: Singapore. *Asia Business, 22*(10), 33-43.

Brian, T. (2003). Using public-private partnerships to fund hotel development projects. *Journal of Retail & Leisure Property, 3*(1), 21-31.

Bull, O.A. (1994). Pricing a motel's location. *International Journal of Contemporary Hospitality Management, 6*(6), 10-15.

Burgess, E.W. (1925). The growth of the city: An introduction to a research project In R.E. Park, E.W. Burgess, & R.D. McKenzie (Eds.). *The city*, (pp. 47-62), Chicago: University of Chicago Press.

Butler, R.W. (1980). The concept of a tourism area cycle of evolution: Implications for the management of resources. *Canadian Geographer, 24*, 5-12.

Chan, W.W., & Lam, J.C. (2001). Environmental costing of sewage discharged by hotels in Hong Kong. *International Journal of Contemporary Hospitality Management, 13*(4/5), 218-227.

Chen, J.J., & Wills, D. (1999). *The impact of china's economic reforms upon land, property, and construction.* UK: Ashgate Publishing Ltd.

Collier, P., & Gregory, A. (1995). *Management accounting in hotel groups.* CIMA, London.

Conner, F.L. (2000). Hoteliers and corporate travel buyers to promote "green" hotels together. *Cornell Hotel and Restaurant Administration Quarterly, 41*(5), 16.

Culligan, P.E. (1990). Looking up: Lodging supply and demand. *Cornell Hotel and Restaurant Administration Quarterly, 31*(2), 32-35.

Dexter, C. (1992). Life cycle models for pacific island destinations. *Journal of Travel Research, 30*(2), 26-32.

Egan, D., & Ball, S. (2004). *The Location of Budget Hotels.* Conference Paper ESRC Urban & Regional Economics Seminar Group.

Egan, D., & Nield, K. (2001). Towards a theory of intraurban hotel location. *Urban Studies, 37*, 611-621.

Egan, D., Knowles, T., & Bey, J. (2000). The location of licensed premises in the UK. *International Journal of Wine Marketing, 12*(1), 5-15.

Fung, K.I., Yan, Z.M., & Ning, Y.M. (1992). Shanghai: China's world city. In Y.M. Yeung, & W. Hu (Eds.). *China's costal cities: Catalysts for modernization* (pp. 124-152). United States: Honolulu University of Hawaii Press.

Gu, H. (1998). Review and prospect of urban planning in Shenzhen, in the Essays by the Urban Planning and Design Institute of Shenzhen, 42-49.

Guseman, P.K. (1988). How to pick the best location. *American Demographics, 10*(8), 42-44.

Harvey, J. (1987) *Urban land economics.* Basingstoke: Macmillan.

Higley, J. (2003). Discounting isn't bad when it's done correctly. *Hotel and Motel Management, 218*(13), 8.

Hsu, H.C.C., & Powers, T. (2002). *Marketing hospitality* (3rd ed.). NJ: John Wiley & Son.

Isard,W. (1956). *Location and space-economy.* Cambridge: MIT Press.

Jagels, M.G., & Coltman, M.M. (2004). *Hospitality management accounting.* NJ: John Wiley & Sons.

Jim, C.Y. (2000). Environmental changes associated with mass urban tourism and nature tourism development in Hong Kong. *Environmentalist, 20*(3), 233.

Kevin, K.F.W., & Lam, C. (2001). Predicting hotel choice decisions and segmenting hotel consumers: A comparative assessment of a recent consumer based approach. *Journal of Travel & Tourism Marketing, 11*(1).

Kivell, P. (1993). *Land and the city.* London: Routledge.

Ling, & Isaac (1994). The development of urban land policy in china. *Property Management, 12*(4), 12-17.

Lockyer, T. (2005). The perceived importance of price as one hotel selection dimension. *Tourism Management, 26*(5), 529-537.

Moutinho, L., & Paton, R. (1991). Site selection analysis in tourism: The LOCAT model. *Service Industries Journal, 11*(1), 1-10.

Northcott, D. (1992). *Capital investment decision making.* London: CIMA.

Pearce, D. (1995). *Tourism today: A geographical analysis.* London: Longman Second Edition.

Plog, S. (2001). Why destinations areas rise and fall in popularity. *Cornell Hotel and Restaurant Administration Quarterly, 42*(3), 13-25.

Richardson, H.W. (1977). *The new urban economics: And alternatives.* London: Pion Limited.

Roubi. S., & Litteljohn, D. (2004). What makes hotel values in the UK? A hedonic valuation model. *International Journal of Contemporary Hospitality Management, 16*(3), 175-181.

Smith, L. (1986). A hard landing awaits Singapore. *Fortune, 113*(2), 97-100.

Song, S., & Zhang, H.K. (2002). Urbanisation and city size distribution in China. *Urban Studies, 39*(12), 2317-2327.

Song, Y. (2003). *Metropolitan areas: Thinking from practice to theory.* China Environment Science Publish house.

Thünen, J.H. von (1826). *Der isolierte Staat in Beziehung auf Landwirtschaft und Nationalökonomie.* Hamburg: Perthes.

Tse, C.E., & West, J.J. (1992). Development strategies for international hospitality markets. In R. Teare, and M. Olsen, (Eds.), *International hospitality management: Corporate strategy in practice.* London: Pitman Publishing.

Wang Fuhai, & Li Guicai (2002). Some points about the characteristics of planning in Shenzhen and its future development: 20th anniversary of SSEZ. *City Planning Review, 24*(8), 24-27 (in Chinese).

Xue Feng, & Zhou Jin (1999). On the reform of urban planning—The establishment of Regulatory Plan & Ordinance in Shenzhen. *Urban Planning Forum, No. 4* (in Chinese).

Zhu Jieming (2003). From land use right to land development right: Institutional change in China's urban development. *Urban Studies, 41*(7), 1249-1267.

Chapter 2

Marketing

Marketing management is:

> . . . the process of analyzing, planning, implementing, coordinating, and controlling programmes involving the conception, pricing, promotion, and distribution of products, services and ideas designed to create and maintain beneficial exchanges with target markets for the purpose of achieving organizational objectives.

(Moutinho, 2000, p. 121)

CHAPTER OBJECTIVES

On completion of this chapter the reader will understand:

- the place that marketing has in the successful operation of a hotel
- the difference between tangible and nontangible marketing
- the approaches taken by management to segment the market and differentiate their product
- the needs, wants, and demands of guests
- the place of emotion in the purchase decision
- the importance of internal marketing
- the ways in which the Internet has changed hotel marketing

The International Hotel Industry: Sustainable Management
© 2007 by The Haworth Press, Inc. All rights reserved.
doi:10.1300/5869_03

Key Word Definitions

competitive analysis: Comparison of the products available from competitors to evaluate one's strengths.

differentiation: The ability to convey to a customer a tangible or intangible advantage of one product over another.

environmental scanning: The analysis of trends that may affect the product offered by a hotel.

internal marketing: Influencing employees to be conscious of the customer, to have a marketing focus and be proactive in promoting sales.

MICE: Meetings, Incentive, Convention & Exhibition.

opportunity analysis: Matching a hotel's product strengths to opportunities while avoiding threats caused by product weaknesses.

salient: Those items that readily come to mind.

segmentation: To divide a large customer base into smaller homogeneous categories based on a variety of applied factors.

service culture: An organization has a culture of giving service.

Chapter Review

The ability to market a hotel in the appropriate way to the appropriate market is essential to the success of the business. For this to succeed, those in key roles need to understand the product that they are selling and the market to which it is being sold. Managers maximize their returns through understanding the market they are operating in and applying those marketing techniques that can best attract guests. This chapter is not intended to cover all aspects of marketing, as there are many good books which do that, but rather to give the reader sufficient depth and stimulation to develop a questioning of the topic. This discussion includes the concepts of segmentation, differentiation, and target marketing and their use as tools to identify the market that is most appropriate for expenditure of marketing resources. Also the concept of internal marketing, a principle sometimes overlooked, is discussed with emphasis on the influence that this principle has on guest/staff interactions.

INTRODUCTION TO THEORY: MARKETING

Hotels are a service industry. Hotel products have the following characteristics: inseparability, intangibility, perishability, and variability. Since the Industrial Revolution, international economies have changed from what was essentially an industrial society to one which is dominated by service industries. This change has been referred to as the "second Industrial Revolution." As society has changed, with people having more disposable income and more free time, there has been a growing awareness and desire by a greater number of people for service-orientated products such as hotels. Of particular note is that these changes, although initiated in the Western world are happening elsewhere around the world, for example, China. With China's massive population, and the opening up of her borders to international travel, very significant impacts will be seen in the hotel industry internationally. Along with this growth, understanding is needed for the products that are being marketed.

THE Ps OF MARKETING

Since the early 1960s many marketers have been using the "4Ps" marketing mix: (1) product, (2) price, (3) promotion, and (4) place. Consideration is given to the change that would result from varying the product, price, promotion, and place in achievement of the organizational goals. However, use of the 4Ps is limiting when considering a service orientated business such as a hotel as it does not adequately reflect the complexity of the product. In response to the limitations of the 4Ps marketing mix, Booms and Bitner (1981) proposed a 7P marketing mix. These 7Ps included the 4Ps, adding participants, physical evidence, and process. Whether there are 6Ps, 7Ps, or 8Ps (Brien & Jeannie, 1993; Magrath, 1986; Collier, 1991) is not important for the purpose of this discussion, but what is of importance is that in the hotel industry, the service characteristics need to be reflected in the approach to marketing. To be able to understand those characteristics it is necessary to comprehend the basic human characteristics of needs, wants, and demands.

NEEDS, WANTS, AND DEMANDS

People, including employees, stakeholders, and guests, are the core component of the hotel industry. A key part of marketing a hotel to the guest requires an understanding of the needs, wants, and demands of the potential and returning guest.

- **Needs**—human beings have many basic needs including food, clothing, safety, feeling of belonging, and so on. When these basic needs are not met the person takes one of two actions: (1) looks for an object that will satisfy the need, or (2) tries to reduce the need. These are influenced by individual personality and culture.
- **Wants**—communication of needs—wants are viewed as things that will satisfy needs.
- **Demands**—buying power of wants—people have many wants, but may only have limited ability to purchase; when a person has the ability to purchase a want it becomes a demand.

Regarding marketing, what approach do you tend to take?

I do most of my own marketing, certainly all of my overseas marketing. I do it because I quite enjoy it and there is nobody that can sell this hotel like I can because it has been part of my life for thirty-five years. Over those years I have learned what the clients want and expect [demand]. Their expectations have grown over the years and the trick is to keep up with those demands.

(Terry Holmes, Executive Director,
The Stafford, London)

The decision to purchase a hotel product normally begins with a need and is affected by some type of stimuli, for example a television commercial, a newspaper advertisement, or the Internet. In many situations the development of a need is a subtle process. Although it may be observed that some people suddenly express that they need something, often this is the outward expression of a developing inner feeling of need.

What are you finding out about the needs of your customers?

What guests are looking for in a room is a very residential feel, 300 count sheets, duvets, a work space that is comfortable (desk, chair), current colors and good feel to the room, upscale bathroom amenities. In public spaces they need a place to work and to socialize that is comfortable.

(Steve Pagano, Hotel Manager,
Marriott Hotel, San Diego)

The development of needs in the consumer is a major component of marketing success. In the selection process, customers make repeated decisions as they continually attempt to satisfy their perceived needs.

Potential customers looking for a hotel room make a number of decisions when choosing where to stay. The process that they go through in the selection of a product is important for hotel management to understand. As suggested by Lewis (1984), management should know (1) that a particular hotel will be evaluated differently by different guests, (2) where a particular guest is satisfied with one hotel they may be dissatisfied with another, and (3) the perceptions of guests change over time and with experience. The decision process by potential guests is a complex process. Lockyer (2005) develops this decision process and suggests the importance of what is referred to as "Trigger Points" in the decision process.

All consumers are not the same, they are influenced by numerous factors such as personality, culture, and so on. When their needs are put into a condition where they can be communicated they then become wants. These are the things that a person perceives as having the power to satisfy their needs. This is the beginning of the search process, and the selection of alternatives that would have the ability to satisfy the need. Although a consumer may identify many needs and wants, not all of these are converted into a demand for a product. As a result of limited ability to purchase, only a few of the needs and wants may be converted into demands. The ability to purchase relates to the many factors that make up the individual, which include such things as age, income, life experience, gender, previous purchase experiences, etc. An important part of the marketing process is therefore to understand those characteristics that make us individuals and to try to recognize this in such a way that there is a large enough market to successfully target. This process is called market segmentation.

How have guest requirements changed?

Over the years, guests have become more sophisticated in their wants and their needs and as the generations come along the demand of the client becomes more because they become far more educated.

(Terry Holmes, Executive Director,
The Stafford, London)

The marketing process does not simply look at demographic issues. There are many other factors which are more difficult to quantify that influence the purchase decision. This could be as simple as the facilities that the guest has at home—in the hotel they expect at least that, and perhaps more.

MARKET SEGMENTATION

Because each guest has unique needs and wants, each guest is potentially a separate market. In a perfect marketing environment a hotel could design a separate marketing product for each guest, this could include the floor level in the hotel, colors used in the decorations, type of pillow, smell of the shampoo, view from the window, size of the television screen, and so on. While this could be possible in, say, a residential hotel, where the booking is for a long period, in reality most hotels experience a large number of guests who stay for relatively short periods of time.

The correct segmentation of the market does influence the profitability of a hotel.

How does your hotel distinguish itself in the market?

The positioning of Waikiki is pretty much anywhere United States. To a great extent it doesn't give you the feel of a resort-like environment because it is so built up. That's the perception of Waikiki and because of that there is a price point that people would pay up to and after that it no longer becomes a value. If you think about going to an island destination, say the Maldives, Phuket, Bali, or Hawaii, the first thing you think about is how close am I going to be to the sand and the water. In Waikiki a good majority of the hotels don't even have the water view—that defines it. There is an image for the destination. Waikiki has fallen prey to that. For us we have almost developed a destination within a destination, but yet when we tell people we are in Oahu, what people think of is Waikiki, so we have to somehow say we use the Waikiki airport but we are not Waikiki.

(Abid Butt, Managing Director,
Turtle Bay Resort, Hawaii)

There are many ways in which the market for a hotel can be segmented. Some hotel managers may view their market simply as two segments, such as "tourist and local" or "foreigners and regulars" (Wearne & Morrison, 1996). Another way of looking at segmenting a market could include steps such as:

1. deciding on what basis the market could be segmented,
2. developing an understanding of the market segment,
3. developing ways in which the segmented market could be measured,
4. positioning the product so that it becomes attractive to the segmented market, and
5. developing a plan of the mix of products to be sold in the segmented market.

However, these approaches do not take into consideration the diversity within each of these segments, and therefore do not give management a clear understanding of the best way to market. The most common approach to market segmentation is a demographic segmentation, such as age, life-cycle stage, gender, and income. Because of the current increase in female business travelers, some properties have found it profitable to make special provisions for this segment of their market.

Are there specific areas of the market that you target?

We have a high percentage of lady executive travelers—managers. Because of this we have designed one floor especially for ladies putting in things that they need, especially makeup remover, and we light candles to give a nice scent.

(Nash Nasihin Ali, General Manager,
Mutiara Hotel, Johor, Malaysia)

However, care must be taken as demographics may be too simplistic in many cases. For a hotel which segments its product in relationship to guest income, a guest who may be considered outside of this segment may wish to stay for a special family event, second honeymoon, or other vacation that would make the higher than affordable cost acceptable for this particular occasion. The segmentation by income could exclude this possible guest.

Is your market segmented?

Again we are lucky to have a hotel like this. We are in the unique situation where during the week we focus on the meeting and business traveler and at the weekend we look at the leisure travel out of Hong Kong and other areas because of our location with the theme parks. We are quite lucky in having the right facilities in the right location for the right market.

(Peter Pollmeier, General Manager,
Crowne Plaza, Shenzhen, China)

When segmenting a market, external factors such as security can also be an important influence. For example, recent international events (i.e., terrorism) have altered the market for many hotels. Security concerns may influence the willingness for a business to hold large conventions.

Have world security issues changed your market segment?

Security is a huge concern. This hotel used to do extremely well as an incentive market from Australia and the United States and Europe and Japan. That segment is gone now—it is zero.

(Octavia Gamarra, General Manager,
Ritz-Carlton Millenia, Singapore)

PRODUCT DIFFERENTIATION

In its simplest form, differentiation means distinguishing your product or service from those offered by your competition, anticipating that the guest will perceive greater utility, possibly better value or better resolution to their demands (Lewis Chambers & Chacko, 1995). In this endeavor it is of importance to realize that the difference may be just perceived by the guest, there may not be any actual difference, and it is not necessary for there to be a difference as long as the guest perceives a difference. As suggested by Lewis Chambers and Chacko (1995, p. 293) these differences "can be very effective when (1) they cannot be easily duplicated, (2) they appeal to a particular need and/or want, and (3) they create an image or impression that goes beyond the specific difference itself."

What impact does differentiation by price have on your hotel market?

If you allow one part of the market to grow and continue to allow $61 rates, then that appeals to someone who is intensely looking for the value. However, there are others who are spending $129, $139, $149; they enjoy the hotel because of the amenities (restaurant, service, pool, etc.). At the same time the person who is looking for the bargains is now looking for the hotel to offer them those same facilities as for guests paying the higher amounts.

(Luis Barrios, General Manager,
Hacienda Hotel, San Diego)

Because much of the product sold to guests by hotels is intangible, the differentiation of a hotel's product involves a process of making an intangible product tangible. If nothing else, differentiation raises awareness in the mind of the guest, and this can lead to a trial of the product being offered. Unfortunately, differentiation can be a fleeting occurrence—what is a point of differentiation today is common tomorrow. This can be seen by looking at such issues as the availability of Internet in hotels, and how quickly its availability has changed from a point of differentiation to an essential part of the hotel facilities.

Have guest expectations regarding facilities changed?

My principle is that we must be different than our competitors. Now every business traveler wants in-room Internet facility. We don't have that at the moment but soon we are signing an agreement with a supplier. We have no choice—Internet is an expectation now.

(Nash Nasihin Ali, General Manager,
Mutiara Hotel, Johor, Malaysia)

Other examples of how hotel companies differentiate can be seen by undertaking a study of their Web sites. For example, the Marriott group has differentiated its products by the use of different messages:

- Marriott Hotels and Resorts: "Going above and beyond"
- JW Marriott Hotels and Resorts: "Discover a hotel that defines a new dimension of luxury"
- Marriott Fairfield Inn: "For travelers who know"

Although the name of Marriott appears in each of these, they are differentiated for different guest requirements.

In this discussion of market segmentation and differentiation of product in hotel marketing, it is often considered better to work toward retaining customers, rather than being overly interested in attracting new customers.

How does differentiation impact upon your returning guests?

Fifty percent of my clients are regulars, they probably come straight to me, they are professionals—they come to the city and they bring their clients, and so they know the staff, everybody is friendly to them, they know what they need. With such a high ratio of my guests being repeat (50 percent), I have to concentrate on keeping them, making sure they are happy. Price is very competitive.

(P. S. Ramdas, Managing Director,
Tourist Home [Pvt.] Ltd, Egmore, Chennai, India)

Research indicates that this approach is less expensive in comparison to continually trying to attract new customers. However this strategy does not adequately consider infrequent customers. Hotels need to develop ways to attract new customers, just as manufacturers of goods have different marketing strategies depending upon if the items are frequently purchased or if they are of a durable nature (Bridges, Ensor, & Raman, 2003).

How do you know when your marketing is successful?

Once we have communicated what the hotel has to offer to everyone out there—a taxi driver when asked what is the best hotel in Singapore, he will say Ritz-Carlton.

(Anton Kilayko, Director, Public Relations,
Ritz-Carlton Millenia, Singapore)

UNDERSTANDING THE FACTORS
GUESTS ARE LOOKING FOR

To be able to segment and differentiate a hotel product, it is necessary to understand what the guest wants. Unfortunately, although many studies have been conducted, there does not seem to be one "right" answer. Guests staying in a hotel have different characteristics and therefore demand different outcomes from their stay, however this is a simplification of the whole question. It is evident from research that a tourist looking for accommodations may put considerable effort into the process of selection (Moutinho, 1986), while a person on a business trip may simply allocate the decision to another person (secretary, administrator, etc.) with little concern as long as a minimum desired standard is achieved. Although there are some clear consistencies in understanding the factors that influence the selection process, for example, age (Phillips & Sternthal, 1977; Kiel & Layton, 1981; Biehal, 1983), even this seemingly straightforward characteristic is not as simple as may be expected. Dolnicar and Otter (2003) reviewed twenty-one journal articles published over the period of 1984-2000 looking at factors influencing occupancy. From these articles Dolnicar and Otter (2003) extracted 173 attributes. These included such factors as image, service, price/value, hotel, room, food and beverage, security, and others. In addition, there has been research into the impact of different parts of the market, for example: American business travelers (Weaver & Oh, 1993), motor coach tour operators (Schaefer, Illum, & Margavio, 1995), leisure, business meetings, conventions (Dube & Renaghan, 1999), and business guests (Lockyer, 2002).

Callan (1996) summarized a number of research projects that had been conducted and of particular interest is the finding that within many of these, the standard of housekeeping and cleanliness was rated as the most important in the selection of accommodations by guests.

How important is guest expectations in your hotel?

Certainly those of us in the luxury market continue to strive to perfect the service that we provide. There is a distinct group of clientele out there who expect high quality, who expect us to handle the details, to anticipate their needs. The better equipped a hotel is in doing that the greater will be the gain from the market place. The typical traveler is very savvy, they have high expectations. We aim to stay ahead of the game. Service is ultimately what determines the success of the hotel. It is wonderful to have beautiful furnishings but ultimately it is people, this continues to be a people industry with perhaps even a continued greater focus on the internal guest and greater realization that taking care of them ultimately means the success of the hotel is guaranteed.

(Linda Wan, General Manager,
Hotel Crescent Court, Dallas)

Do different groups of guests have different expectations?

In the Japanese market the most important thing in the hotel is cleanliness. If they perceive that the hotel is not clean they will not come back. Cleanliness is next to godliness in Japan, more than for any other country where I have been.

(Octavia Gamarra, General Manager,
Ritz-Carlton Millenia, Singapore)

This would lead management to the view that cleanliness is the most important factor that guests are looking for. The importance of cleanliness has also been identified more recently by Lockyer (2002). In these studies, "price or room rate" were not rated highly by potential guests as a deciding factor in the selection of accommodations. In addition, research has shown that there is a gap between what accommodation managers *believe* is important and what guests *say* is important in the selection of accommodations (Lockyer, 2002). One reason for this lack of understanding is the research implements used. For example, Saleh and Ryan (1992) used factor analysis; Dube and Renaghan (2000) used frequency tables; Weaver and Oh (1993) used mean values and group comparisons; Tsaur and Gwo-Hsiung (1995) used descriptive statistics, to illustrate a few. Each of these researchers has developed a list of attributes, using a variety of methods, and then asked potential guests to rank the identified attributes. This approach has raised a number of problems, as identified by Callan (1996) where cleanliness is identified as the most important attribute. The potential customer participating in the research has little or no idea before staying in a particular establishment as to the level of its cleanliness. However, cleanliness is a factor which has an impact on whether the guest returns and on levels of repeat business. Guest satisfaction and expectation have a twofold effect on occupancy, first they affect the repeat purchasing decisions, and second they affect the guest desire to satisfy their expectations. There is no quantifiable relationship between these two (McDougall & Levesque, 1994).

Research by Lockyer (2005) into understanding the important factors suggests a different perspective, where some factors are essential and other factors are trigger points. For example, price may be of high importance in one situation while in another situation it may not. As discussed in the chapter on location, if a person important to you were in the hospital and you needed to visit at short notice, then price of accommodations may be far less important than if you were part of an amateur sports team wishing to attend a tournament. While price may be a trigger point in this example, cleanliness is an essential expectation. This further emphasizes the complexity of trying to segment or differentiate the hotel guest market.

EMOTION AND THE PURCHASE DECISION

Part of the process to successfully market an intangible product is to develop an emotional relationship between the guest and the hotel. Research by Barsky and Nash (2002, p. 39) looked at this question and resolved that "emotionally connected guests are more likely to return to a hotel. . . ." They also discovered that "the sets of key loyalty-inducing emotions are slightly different for each industry segment, although feeling comfortable figures strongly in most of them." Therefore the emotions that a guest has influences the possibility that the guest will return to stay again at a particular hotel. Emotions are inherently difficult to understand and are subject to change.

An example of this is the way in which the tragedy of September 11, 2001, has influenced the market segments of hotels:

How has your market segment changed over the past couple of years?

After September 11, we had to rethink the way we do hotels. We have now a driving market (people come from Northern California, Arizona, Los Angeles). People don't want to fly so they will drive. This market here, although competitive, has high demand, which is good and so rates are well maintained.

(Luis Barrios, General Manager,
Hacienda Hotel, San Diego)

The emotional impact of the terrorist attacks has resulted in many more of this hotel's guests traveling by car, for safety reasons, bringing about a change in the market. The marketing of the hotel product since 9/11 is being handled differently, marketing to guests in regions that are within reasonable driving distances from the hotel, having available car parking space, understanding that this may result in arrival time and departure times being different from other market segments, and understanding the family makeup of those traveling by car. An additional issue that this change also illustrates is that when a hotel's guest drives to a property, the choices available to them are greatly extended. They are no longer limited by flying to a destination and getting a taxi to a particular hotel, but on the way to a destination may pass many competing properties that could satisfy their needs.

INTERNAL MARKETING

Within the hotel industry the interrelationship between the guest and the employees is important. It is in part the quality of this relationship in what is referred to as the service encounter that makes the sale (Crosby, Evans, & Cowles, 1990). Internal marketing is a philosophy for managing personnel and a systematic way of developing and enhancing a service culture. As staff members interact with people there are many unspoken responses that become part of the message which is communicated. Because of the importance of the relationship between a hotel's employee and the guest, the spoken and unspoken responses become integral to guest satisfaction. All employees within a hotel who have any contact with a guest have the ability to influence the guest experience either positively or negatively.

Do you have an example of a staff member providing outstanding service?

There was a couple staying in the hotel who were going to get married while jumping out of an aeroplane. They had to have a witness jump out of the plane with them, and their best man was to do this. The day before the best man withdrew and so they couldn't get married. The concierge volunteered and he jumped with the guests so their plans could be fulfilled.

(Linda Wan, General Manager,
Hotel Crescent Court, Dallas)

How do staff/guest relationships influence internal marketing?

You raise the level of delight—the reaction the guest will have is unbelievable and they will certainly remember the experience. That is what you are trying to strive for. For example, a guest brings their child to the hotel, you know the name and the date of birth of the child. You surprise the child in the room with a birthday cake. This child happens to like Mickey Mouse. So the rooms' service staff member comes in an outfit dressed as Mickey Mouse. When the guests finish in the restaurant, they get back to the room and there is Mickey Mouse standing in the room. Now that they will remember.

(Robert Lagerwey, Assistant Hotel Manager & F&B,
Ritz-Carlton Millenia, Singapore)

Employees indicate in many unspoken ways how they feel about the company, these include if the employee likes the kind of work they are doing, if the work gives a sense of accomplishment, if they are proud of the company they work for, the overall physical work conditions, feeling good about the future of the company, and an understanding of the business strategy (Rucci, Kirn, & Quinn, 1998). It is evident that many hotels use a number of different approaches to accomplish a positive relationship between staff and guest. The objective is to build employees who have loyalty and an interest in the job that they are doing, and have a desire to develop a customer relationship. An important part of this is the attraction and retention of good staff, and to make sure the employee is motivated. It is interesting to note that employees often treat the customers the same way that they are treated by their management.

What do you do to show staff they are valued?

There are a lot of activities. We as a hotel provide all the benefits and the programs and the recognition to the staff, not what we as a senior management feel is important, but what they are truly looking for. Hopefully we can gather information from the suggestion pool or from surveys and talking to them and getting to know them. Once you have determined what is important to them you find that really it is mainly recognition and it may not necessarily be monetary, it may not be an item, it's often the pat on the back, the "thank you," or "how is your family?" that makes the difference to them.

(Linda Wan, General Manager,
Hotel Crescent Court, Dallas)

Employees convey an important message to the guest. Management can work to develop that relationship so the staff members reflect that positive image. In the chapters on empowerment and human resource management there are examples of how companies are promoting employee relationships and internal marketing.

MARKETING RESEARCH AND INTELLIGENCE

Marketing research is important in environmental scanning, competitive analysis, and opportunity analysis. The important point here is to discover the problems and demands that guests have, and at the same time find out about the competition. It is difficult to simply ask a guest what they want or what the problem may be, as they may not know. Research is developed to study how the guest uses the hotel, and to determine which factors promote or discourage its use or continued use.

Market research is necessary

- to replace intuition with facts;
- to lessen uncertainty;
- to allow a hotel to stay current;
- to endeavor to locate segments of the market;
- to plan for the future; and
- to make business decisions.

Research can identify important product relationships.

What have you found from market research?

Our research into occupancy levels shows that the higher the price, the higher the quality, the higher the occupancy. There is a very clear correlation there.

(Chris Collier, CEO,
Lake District Tourist Board, Cumbria, England)

Some of the areas where research can be undertaken include:

- guest likes and dislikes
- guest characteristics–demographics
- need for new or modified products

- awareness of competition
- guest opinions, beliefs, attitudes, intentions, and behaviors
- demand analysis

To be effective, research does not necessarily have to involve complex data collection and analysis.

What market research do you undertake?

In the evening when you drive past, always look into other hotels. If there are lights on in a lot of rooms then you can estimate their occupancy. I can look at the hotel and tell how well they are doing. My work boys come here, and I ask them. If I see a neighbor I will ask him how things are going. Sometimes they do not tell you right—I go by in the evening and I know things are not as they were reported.

(P. S. Ramdas, Managing Director,
Tourist Home [Pvt.] Ltd, Egmore, Chennai, India)

A great deal can be gained by management's and staff's personal observations.

Another technique for the gathering of marketing information is the use of a quantitative research tool. This type of research deals with numbers. It measures quantitatively what people say, think, perceive, feel, and do. One form of this is the guest feedback type of survey placed in most hotel rooms. The problem with such surveys is not only the way the questions are asked, but research has shown that there are basically two types of people who fill in a survey: those who are very happy with the service, etc., provided and those who are unhappy. It is similar to having a meal in a restaurant: you are often asked at some point, "How did you like the meal?"—many people who did not like the meal would simply smile and not express their true feelings. Quantitative surveys are often used because of:

- low cost of administrating;
- speed of data collection;
- the situation in which the survey is conducted can be controlled;
- direct contact with guests; and
- new creative ideas.

Qualitative research is designed to obtain guest information on attitudes and behavior on a subjective basis and is a lot more expensive to conduct. There can be problems with generalizing the findings from an often small sample to the population. However, there are advantages as the freedom for respondents to express their own ideas can reveal fresh new issues. For example, a well-organized focus group may raise questions that may never have been considered or thought of if a quantitative survey only was used. Therefore, survey design and data collection need to take a holistic approach.

HOTELS.COM

Internet companies, such as hotels.com, have changed the marketing of hotels throughout the world. Many of these sites emphasize price as a major criterion to people searching for a hotel in a particular location. This has led to an overdominance of consideration of price in the selection of hotels.

What is the number one current major issue which is important to you?

The main issue today in the United States is the third-party Internet engines, the hotels.coms. Somehow they have taken away a lot of the control from us where it comes to revenues. We have had to go with them, to give them whatever they need to do business do finally it has become an issue where we lost control.

What are you doing to try to get the control back in your hands?

We are following the steps of the big companies that are booking business on the Web sites. If you want to get the discounts from the big companies you have to go their Web sites so we are shifting to that mentality. We are managing our own Web site and through that offering value to our customers.

Does the size of the hotel make a difference?

There are some small companies who do not know what is going on, and they give all they have to the hotels.com type companies. The big ones (Hilton, Marriot) have a different approach.

(Luis Barrios, General Manager,
Hacienda Hotel, San Diego)

The driving force is now to try and make sure potential guests visit a hotel's own Web site, and to book there as well. This has the effect of taking the dominant focus away from price, and allows the hotel to sell the product in a way which is appropriate to the particular establishment.

Do you agree with the statement that one of the worst things that the industry did was to teach people to expect discounts?

Yes—A to expect discounts and B to give the control of their inventory to an outside source. You must control your own inventory. If you give your inventory to companies like Expedia, Travelocity—they can sell it at what they want. Once you do that you have lost control of your business.

(Terry Holmes, Executive Director,
The Stafford, London)

There is no doubt that Web sites such as hotels.com will continue to have a large influence on the hotel market, but over time as more and more properties get back their control on the sale of their product, this may change. This will also come as hotels try to educate their guests that the best deal can be obtained from their Web sites.

SUMMARY

This chapter has discussed the marketing of the hotel product and the place marketing has in the successful operation of a hotel. The chapter began with a discussion of the basic concepts of marketing including guest needs, wants, and demands. Of particular importance is the process that a potential guest goes through in the selection of a hotel and how a particular product may be segmented for specific markets. Because customers are all different with a myriad of differing motivations, many hotels have a number of different "brands" that are focused on specific parts of the market.

A major issue discussed in this chapter is that of Internet marketing. For managers, this has become very complex and in some ways a negative experience. Managing the pricing and sales strategies on the Internet is as a major challenge for managers. To be able to market a property appropriately, managers need to have the right information about the market at the right time; this involves research and an understanding of what is happening in the market so that the hotel's product can be correctly placed in the market.

DISCUSSION

A. Why is it not enough to try and sell the hotel product just as you would a box of nails or bolts? Identify why there may be a difference.
B. Identify on the Internet two or more hotel products and determine if you can detect what segments of the market they are aimed at, also see if you can identify any differentiation of the product offered.
C. What actions can you take to promote internal marketing among your employees?
D. What actions can you take to control the presence of discount pricing on a hotels.com-type Web site?
E. Investigate a few hotels in your region and evaluate at least four ways in which they use segmentation and differentiation in their product.
F. Investigate sources of secondary data that would be helpful to you as a manager of a large international hotel.

CASE STUDIES

Case 2.1. MICE Market in Singapore

Within Singapore there has been a lot of analysis into the MICE market—(Meetings Incentive Conventions Exhibits). Overall this segment is a lot more profitable for a hotel. Overall there is a higher average rate, plus people attending such events tend to spend lot more in food and beverage. As a comparative, if there is a room occupied by a business traveler and one occupied by a meeting attendee, overall there is additional revenue of about 24 percent from the person attending the meeting.

Many hotels in Singapore were designed for large conventions. However, the MICE market is now looking for facilities for between 70 and 150 attendees. A major reason for this is that with the technology available, it is no longer necessary for everyone to meet. Department heads or division heads would attend meetings rather than all employees. To take advantage of this, hotels are trying to increase their available rooms suitable for meetings. Unfortunately at this hotel we originally built also to have large conferences, and our ball-room that can hold 1,000 people, cannot be divided, which makes it is just too large for most current conferences. In this hotel, we are in the process of try-ing to increase the meeting rooms in the hotel by converting space on the third floor into meeting space which will give two additional rooms. High ceil-ings and good natural light are both important to this market. Another move the hotel is making is to moving the tennis courts so that the space can be used for a second ballroom. Because of the lack of meeting space it was re-ported that the hotel had recently turned down close to $7 million worth of business because the meeting rooms were already booked. They are trying to organize more meeting rooms to accommodate requests.

Roger Lagerwey, Hotel Manager,
Ritz-Carlton Millenia, Singapore

Questions

1. As general manager of a large international hotel how would you eval-uate short-term MICE needs in comparison to long term MICE needs?
2. Evaluate two or three hotels in your area and compare their marketing segment as it relates to MICE. Can you identify any differences?
3. What segmentation opportunities are available to a hotel in relation to MICE?

Case 2.2. "I Have That at Home"

The Cumbria Tourist Board *represents England's tourism industry on a whole range of policy, strategy, and regulatory issues. It firmly believes in tak-ing an evidence-based approach to tourism management, development, and marketing. It oversees the English Lake District, which boasts some of Brit-ain's most beautiful countryside. The variety of spectacular mountains, peace-ful lakes, rolling fells, and bustling market towns make the Lake District a unique part of Britain. The following came from an interview with the CEO:*
The rating of hotels by external bodies where boxes are ticked if items are found is too generalized and does not give a good indication of overall quality. I am much more concerned about the "touchy feely" bits, the bits that excite and exceed expectations, and the delight factors. How you measure them is much harder. To overcome all the constraints in the existing schemes we looked at having a design-led approach to excellence and quality because so many of our businesses are actually appealing to that market, rather than people looking for cheap. The industry in the Lakes have got into a mindset which says, "The national park wants to preserve us as a Victorian destina-tion, so we will preserve our accommodation as a Victorian type of a desti-nation as well" so you get the chintz and you get dark rooms, old-fashioned

lighting. There was an operator who had bought a new property and done some refurbishing. I went in to have a look and he was very proudly showing me. We got back down to the hallway that was dark, Edwardian, and I said are you going to do this, are you going to lift this? He said, No, I have done this, I want to preserve the ambience of the Victorian country residence. I wondered if he really knew what he was doing. I went away and thought about it. Visitors are coming here because they love the lakes and the mountains, they are not consciously thinking, "I want a Victorian experience, I am going to the Lakes and book into a nice little Victorian type of hotel." Visitors still want accommodation that exceeds what they have at home. Now you already have a very high quality, certainly in this country. You have already thrown out your chintz and you have gone down a much more contemporary line. To come away and go back into that is not particularly satisfying unless it is done incredibly well, far better than you could ever aspire to yourself. You have to keep above that because where is the capacity to delight if all that you are providing is what they have at home. That is why we brought in some key designers who were top of the field, and asked them to look at different factors and come up with what they would do with that sector. We didn't give them the mediocre stuff where even I could walk in and say get rid of the candlewick bedspreads and frilly curtains. That's too easy. We gave them the very best that we had in Cumbria at the time and said what would you do to that to make it better. That is why it is called "Better than the Best." This was the first part of the plan.

Part 2 would be that we would draw down some funding from government and invite people to bid to receive the funding so that they have some cash to match what they were going to do with refurbishment so that they can accelerate the change but in return for having the cash to do that, we would be saying to them, "Yes, but to get the money you must have a staff training program, you must have a proper business plan, you must be engaged in a marketing system so that your product is on display the world over; you must be part of the visitor pay-back scheme that the tourism and conservation department runs. Then you are not just improving results, the quality of the product, you are lifting everything against a whole series of parameters."

Christine Collier, Chief Executive Officer
Cumbria Tourist Board
Cumbria, England

Questions

1. Suggest ways in which you may be able to measure the "touchy feely bits."
2. What are some of the threats of maintaining the Victorian marketing approach?
3. What role, if any, do you think that governments, both national and local, have in the marketing development of hotels?

Case 2.3. Two Hotels in the Lake District*

The Abbey Hotel

Near to where I live in the north of England are two hotels, about three ki-lometers apart. Both are close to the same Lake and so have similar oppor-tunities for rambling and for sailing. Both are close to road junctions and have good road access. Both have countryside locations with good views from many rooms of the local hills and moorlands. Both have an***AA rating. AA ratings are the most recognized form of hotel grading in Britain.

Let us call the first hotel "The Abbey Hotel." This is how it describes itself in its own brochure.

Overlooking the Lake and some of England's finest fells, the Abbey Hotel offers the warmest of welcomes and leisure facilities that provide the oppor-tunity to unwind after a long day. With easy access to the motorway, and a main line station 20 miles away, the hotel offers a good base for meetings and small conferences. It specializes in catering for team building courses for businesses and is a great base from which to launch in to the hills.

We offer a wide range of activities ideal for entertaining clients, product launches, encouraging team bonding, or just having fun and getting to know each other. And you don't always have to be "meeting room bound" as we have joined forces with our specialist partners, to provide a host of fun and existing activities—such as: Corporate golf days, archery, after dinner speak-ers, quad bikes, trivia quiz, and so on.

Guests can enjoy a delicious and extensive menu in The Sonnets Res-taurant or a more relaxed snack within the Lakers Bar, which is also a great place to unwind at the end of a long day. Leisure facilities include a 14-meter indoor swimming pool, Jacuzzi, sauna, steam room, full gymnasium, bad-minton, table tennis, and lawn tennis. On-site mountain bike hire is also available. Cyclists and horse riders will love the forest trails.

Enjoy a short break that's just that little bit different. As well as relaxing in great surroundings and enjoying excellent wining and dining, we offer you entertainment in a number of guises. You may find yourself in the middle of a crime scene at one of our "Murder Mystery" dinners or want to join in a great cabaret evening. The hotel is bright and stylish with an enthusiastic ap-proach to service and a commitment to get the simple things right . . . every time. Good honest standards from people who genuinely care about making your stay special.

Price: UK £48 per person per night for bed and breakfast.
Special price: £37 per person per night for bed and breakfast.
Features: Number of bedrooms: 48, Number of meeting rooms: 6,
    Meeting room capacity: 150.

---

*This case study was kindly provided by a University lecturer who lives in the Lake District of England. (To maintain anonymity, assumed names have been used for the ho-tels in this case study.)

The Partridge Inn

Let us call the second hotel "The Partridge Inn." This is how it describes it-self in its own brochure.

> The Partridge is a charming old Coaching Inn situated close to the lake in an unspoilt part of the north of England. It is one of the last remaining traditional local hostelries with its unique period atmosphere, sense of timelessness, and peaceful location. The history of The Partridge stretches back over 500 years. Originally a farmhouse, it was converted over 200 years ago to a popular Alehouse. You cannot escape the sense of being surrounded by history the moment you walk in the door.

The Partridge enjoys a well-deserved international reputation. Our discerning guests return year after year to relish The Partridge's timeless elegance and understated luxury. Those who visit us for the first time are instantly captivated by its historic charm and grace, redolent of tradition and a bygone era, tempered by essential modern comforts. Our bar is one of the best known in the area. The mellow, polished walls and oak settles create an atmosphere in which to enjoy a convivial drink in relaxing surroundings. With real log fires in the lounges, stunning fresh flower arrangements, exposed beams, period furniture, and polished parquet flooring, the lounges are the epitome of a true hostelry.

The fifteen individually decorated bedrooms have been sympathetically and completely refurbished to the highest standard. Three suite type rooms have been created offering extra space and a comfortable sitting area within the bedroom. The new bathrooms are considered to be amongst the best available and have both a bath and a powerful shower. Beautiful fabrics and antique pieces combine to maintain that unique atmosphere. We of course offer an early morning tea service. The high standard of food served at The Partridge is very well known, both to local diners and to our guests from further afield. Ranging from local specialties to fine dining there is something to suit all tastes. An extensive choice of wines from around the world complements the daily changing menus. Staying at the Partridge Inn is a relaxing experience offering excellent accommodation and superb food in magnificent surroundings. There are many attractions to see and explore including beautiful walks from the doorstep and famous lakes.

For the more sporting minded, there is a great links golf course nearby for which we can arrange tee times. We are within easy reach of historic market towns and can also help you organize fishing on the local rivers and lakes and shooting on two of the local estates. The Partridge can accommodate you in a stylish yet traditional manner.

> Price: UK £72 per person per night for bed and breakfast.
> Special price: UK £225 per person for three night bed, breakfast, and evening meal.

When I go to the Abbey Hotel, the first thing I notice is the car park, which is wrapped around two sides of the hotel. In the car park are very large temporary hoardings advertising cabaret nights over the next month or two. Inside, the reception area is clean but looks due for re-decoration. The two rooms we are staying in are almost identical, certainly with same patterned wallpaper and patterned carpets. They are warm, comfortable and have little personality. The dining room is large and the tables laid out in long rows. The tables are neatly laid and have a small decoration on them in the form of some fabric flowers. Our breakfast is self-serve, with fruit juices, cereals, bread, toast, tea, and coffee available. The bar serves well-known international brands of beers. The staff and the service are both competent. The swimming pool and the gymnasium are both modern and well fitted out, though there are few staff in evidence. The changing rooms are overdue for cleaning and have a slightly strange smell.

When I go to the Partridge Inn, the first thing I notice is the building itself: A long two-storey building clearly of considerable age. There is still a mounting block, which is a set of stone steps used in the past to help riders mount their horses. Inside, there are glass cases hung in the entrance displaying local exhibits and the smell of lilies is evident. The two rooms we are staying in are quite different in shape and decoration—my room has an antique walnut desk with matching chair. The dining room is small and intimate, each table lit with a candle and with fresh flowers. We order breakfast from a menu and are pleased to have the choice of traditional cooked breakfasts including smoked fish and even kedgeree (a lightly curried rice and fish recipe). The service is polite, attentive and cheerful. We take morning coffee in a guest lounge in which the only noise is the gentle ticking of a grandfather clock.

Brian Eaton, Senior Lecturer in Tourism,
University of Central Lancashire, Carlisle, England

Questions

1. Describe what the two hotels share as a product offering, and what is different.
2. What is the primary market, and secondary markets for each hotel?
3. Describe a typical group staying at the hotel—how many in the group, the ages of the group, their relationship with each other, how long they might stay, what their activities might be.
4. Why do hotels run special offers?
5. If both hotels have an AA3*** grading and are located close together, why do they not charge the same price?
6. What is the difference between grading, standards, and quality?
7. What does this tell us about concepts of quality?

REFERENCES

Barsky, J., & Nash, L. (2002). Evoking emotion: Affective keys to hotel loyalty. *Cornell Hotel and Restaurant Administration Quarterly, 43*(1), 39-46.

Biehal, G.J. (1983). Consumers prior experiences and perceptions in auto repair choice. *Journal of Marketing, 47*(Summer), 82-91.

Booms, B., & Bitner, M.J. (1981). Marketing strategies and organizational structures for service firms. In J Donnely & W. George (Eds.), Marketing of Services, (pp. 47-51). Chicago: American Marketing Association.

Bridges, E., Ensor, K.B., & Raman, K. (2003). The impact of need frequency on service marketing strategy. *The Service Industry Journal, 23*(3), 40.

Brien, E., & Jeannie, M. (1993). Six Ps for four characteristics: A complete positioning strategy for the professional service firm. *Journal of Professional Services Marketing, 9*(1), 129-146.

Callan, R.J. (1996). An appraisement of UK business travelers' perceptions of important hotel attributes. *Hospitality Research Journal, 19*(4), 113-127.

Collier, D.A. (1991). New marketing mix stresses service. *The Journal of Business Strategy, 12*(2), 42-48.

Crosby, L.A., Evans, K.R., & Cowles. (1990). Relationship quality in services selling: An interpersonal influence perspective. *Journal of Marketing, 54*(July), 68-81.

Dolnicar, S., & Otter, T. (2003). Which hotel attributes matter? A review of previous and a framework for further research. In T. Griffin, & R. Harris (Eds.), *Asia Pacific Tourism Association 9th Annual Conference.* Sydney, Australia. 176-188.

Dube, L., & Renaghan, L.M. (1999). How hotel attributes deliver the promised benefits. *Cornell Hotel and Restaurant Administration Quarterly, 40*(5), 89-95.

Dube, L., & Renaghan, L.M. (2000). Creating visible customer value—How customers view best-practice champions. *Cornell Hotel and Restaurant Administration Quarterly, 41*(1), 62-72.

Kiel, G.C., & Layton, R.A. (1981). Dimensions of consumer information seeking. *Journal of Marketing Research, 18*(May), 233-239.

Lewis, O.K. (1984). Theoretical and practical considerations in research design. *Cornell Hotel & Restaurant Administration Quarterly, 24*(4), 25-35, 28.

Lewis, R.C., Chambers, R.E., & Chacko, H. (1995). *Marketing leadership in hospitality: Foundations and practice* (2nd Ed.). New York: Van Nostrand Reinhold.

Lockyer, T. (2002). Business guest accommodation selection: The view from both sides. *International Journal of Contemporary Hospitality Management, 14*(6), 294-300.

Lockyer, T. (2005). Understanding the dynamics of the hotel purchase decision. *International Journal of Contemporary Hospitality Management, 17*(6), 481-492.

Magrath, A.J. (1986). When marketing services, 4Ps are not enough. *Business Horizons, 29*(3), 44-51.

McDougall, G.H.G., & Levesque, T.J. (1994). A revised view of service quality dimensions: An empirical investigation. *Journal of Professional Service Marketing, 11*(1), 189-209.

Moutinho, L. (1986). Consumer behavior in tourism. *Management Bibliographies and Reviews, 12*(3), 3-42.

Moutinho, L. (2000). Segmentation, targeting, positioning, and strategic marketing. In L. Moutinho, (Ed.), *Strategic management in tourism* (p. 121). Oxon UK: CAB International.

Phillips, L.W., & Sternthal, B. (1977). Age differences in information processing: A perspective on the aged consumer. *Journal of Marketing Research, 14* (November), 444-457.

Rucci, A.J., Kirn, S.P., & Quinn R.T. (1998). The employee-customer-profit chain at Sears. *Harvard Business Review, 76*(1), 82-97.

Saleh, F., & Ryan, C. (1992). Client perceptions of hotels, a multi-attribute approach. *Tourism Management,* (June), 163-168.

Schaefer, A., Illum, S., & Margavio, T. (1995). The relative importance of hotel attributes to motorcoach tour operators. *Journal of Hospitality and Leisure Marketing,* 3, 65-80.

Tsaur, H., & Gwo-Hsiung, T. (1995). Multiattribute decision making analysis for customer preference of tourist hotels. *Journal of Travel and Tourism Marketing,* 4, 55-69.

Wearne, N., & Morrison, A. (1996). *Hospitality marketing.* London: Butterworth-Heinemann Ltd.

Weaver, P.A., & Oh, H.C. (1993). Do American business travellers have different hotel service requirements? *International Journal of Contemporary Hospitality Management, 5*(3), 16-21.

Chapter 3

Human Resources

We would rather employ no-one than employ the wrong person.

Lynette Lesslar,
Ritz-Carlton Millenia, Singapore

CHAPTER OBJECTIVES

On completion of this chapter the reader will understand:

- the nature of employment in the hotel industry
- the impact of social changes on employment in the hotel industry
- the way in which the human resource of a hotel influences occupancy
- the relationship between training and customer loyalty
- the expectations of hotel employees
- the way in which some management groups refer to their employees, and the impact of such action
- the impact of the extended working week
- the issues of staff turnover and recruitment
- the use of job rotation and its role in enhancing employment
- the use of training courses; cost and productivity

Key Word Definitions

human resources: The employees of a hotel being viewed as a resource of that business.

motivation: The driving force behind actions.

The International Hotel Industry: Sustainable Management
© 2007 by The Haworth Press, Inc. All rights reserved.
doi:10.1300/5869_04

part-time employee: Someone who does not work full time; depending on the country there are different legal definitions of what a part-time employee is and the legal requirements to employ someone.

seasonality: Fluctuations in a business demand caused by external factors.

staff turnover: The process of employees/staff leaving and new employees/staff joining an organization.

Chapter Review

In this chapter human resource management indicates the inclusion of the following three elements as identified by Singh (1992, p. 127):

- The activities of traditional personnel management (e.g., recruitment, training, remuneration, discipline).
- A specific managerial and organizational "philosophy" that views people as (1) the major organizational asset; and (2) regards workers as instinctively willing and able to be developed.
- Integration of the personnel management functions into the strategic management of the organization.

This chapter deals with human resource management in an international perspective. While many principles and practices are similar internationally, there are some distinctive differences which will be explored in this chapter. Awareness of such issues broadens understanding of human resources.

What is your approach to human resource management?

Anybody can build a hotel, if you have the money. But it is an inanimate object, just bricks and mortar and then you put in nice carpets and paintings, but it is still just a building. It can be a mausoleum. It is the people who work in it that give it the soul. One of the things I always remember when I was at the Dorchester—I started there in the kitchen. The managing director of the hotel, if he was walking down the corridor and you were coming the other way, he would always open the door and say, "After You." That stuck in my mind, and he was the man that ruled with respect and I think that is what you have to do in most businesses, but if you are in the people business it is even more necessary.

(Terry Holmes, Executive Director,
The Stafford, London, England)

As a business, a hotel's major asset is its employees. The process of recruiting, selection, training, and so on, is expensive and requires considerable care.

How do you view the importance of employment of staff?

If you were thinking about buying new laundry equipment and having an expenditure of half a million dollars for some washers and dryers, can you imagine the amount of time that would be spent scrutinizing the equipment, getting quotes looking at the suppliers, and so on? When looking at a capital expenditure of half a million dollars for ovens, we spend months in the research and looking. When you hire a waiter or a chamber maid and you think that they will be with you for ten years, that is a half million dollar investment by the time you add all the salary, training, and other costs together.

(Christopher Norton, General Manager,
Four Seasons, Singapore)

This chapter discusses the type of employees who work within hotels, the impact that full- and part-time employment has, the way in which employees influence the service quality, and more directly, the occupancy of the hotel. In addition, important issues such as staff turnover, recruitment, training, and the costs relating to these, along with other issues such as employee expectations, the impact that the working week has, and job rotation will also be discussed. The human resource issues are essential to the profitable sustained operation of a hotel.

INTRODUCTION TO THEORY: HUMAN RESOURCES

Because of the characteristics of the hotel industry, human resources is a vital part of its management. Many of the staff in a hotel have a direct relationship with the guests, often not in a directly supervised environment. Managers need to motivate their staff to undertake many complex tasks in a way which will satisfy guests, thereby providing a successful outcome for the stakeholders. To accomplish this, continual training programs need to be in place to ensure staff is well trained in a job which often involves long hours and can be considered to be not particularly attractive. Because of the seasonality and changing demand for staff, hotels often have to rely on temporary and part-time people to fill their staffing requirements.

PART-TIME EMPLOYEES

International research (Cho & Wong, 2001) indicates that a lot of jobs within hotels are filled by employees who are there on a part-time basis. In many parts of the world, work in the hotel industry is viewed as something you do while at university or while you are looking for another job. There are a number of negatives associated with part-time employees in a hotel:

- Employees who are part-time often do not have the level of commitment to service and quality that a full-time employee may have.
- The increased turnover of staff impacts on training costs and other related expenses to the hotel.
- Staff can have a lack of commitment to the success of the hotel in the long term (Stamper & Van Dyne, 2003).
- Managers perceive that part-time employees are less valuable than full-time employees (Inman & Enz, 1995).

Despite such negatives, there is an important place for part-time employees (Guerrier & Lockwood, 1989), as illustrated in the following:

How do you manage seasonality?

Our occupancy fluctuates a lot, we may run at 100 percent for four days and then it may be 30 percent for three days and then 100 percent for nine days. The staffing and their motivation can be a little challenging. Because of the large fluctuation in the occupancy there is also a large variety in the number of staff required. We have a core of full-time employees, and then we use a lot of part-time college students, on-call people. Even though it does make staffing, training, and motivation a little more difficult, we have one major advantage. This is the nicest place in town to work so it is not as difficult as it could be. The part-time employees know they are coming to a beautiful building and we try to match that with the way we treat people so it is not as difficult for me as it would be for managers in other situations.

(Bruce Fery, General Manager,
Grand America, Salt Lake City)

As a contrast to the normal perception of part-time employees, research by Inman and Enz (1995, p. 70) revealed that "critical work attitudes and behavior were as strongly exhibited by part-time workers as by full-time workers, including such measures as competence, work ethic, attendance, and acceptance of organizational standards and values."

Part-time employees in a number of countries are able to work only a stipulated number of hours per week (e.g., twenty). Often, part-time employees do not receive the same benefits as full-time employees, and the difference needs to be made clear. Although part-time employees tend to perform the same tasks and hold the same types of responsibilities as full-time employees, it is often the belief of managers in hotels that part-time employees have a lower commitment to the organization and are less willing to contribute than full-time employees. These ssumptions may influence the way in which they treat their part-time employees. However, there is little empirical evidence to support the assumption that part-time employees are less motivated or committed to the organization (Stamper & Van Dyne, 2003).

What do you see as the major challenges in human resources?

It is not what it was years ago when people were more dedicated to their job. Our challenge now is to change the modern mentality. We are in the service industry. You have to be polite, you have to be courteous, you have to say "Yes." It becomes a great challenge to human resource practitioners to change the mentality. In a big city like Johor the attitude is such that jobs are so plentiful, easy to get. You could resign from this hotel and join another tomorrow. In earlier times when you took a job, you really treasured it and you stayed in that job for a long time. Nowadays, people say if I don't do a good job, so what, I can go to the next hotel. People think if I am waiter here, I can go there and be a captain. Also, we need to change the mentality among our young Malaysians; many are not very interested to work in a service industry, the commitment is not there.

Hotels have always been associated with vices, prostitution, and sleazy night clubs. Not only do we have to change the workers we also have to change the mentality of their parents, because they do not see working in a hotel as a suitable career for their sons and daughters.

In addition there is the wages. To be honest it is pretty low pay compared to someone who joins another kind of industry. It is also esteemed as a very low paid kind of job with long hours. This also does not go well with parents. The turn over is so high, roughly about 25 percent. I spend effort upgrading the associates (we don't call them staff any more).

(Nash Nasihin Ali, General Manager,
Mutiara Hotel, Johor, Malaysia)

EDUCATION AND EMPLOYEES

It is often stated that many part- and full-time hotel employees have a low level of education, but this is an oversimplification. The level of education of the local population has an impact upon the pool from which staff for a hotel can be selected. Around the world there is a similar problem but the ways in which local businesses deal with it are somewhat different. In developing and developed countries levels of education within society are improving. As the level of education increases in the local population, there is a growing reluctance to work in a hotel, as there are other employment opportunities available which give better returns for time invested.

Do you have difficulties recruiting staff?

Nowadays no one wants to work in the hotel industry because young people want to work from nine to five and have Saturday and Sunday off. In a hotel, you must work Saturday and Sunday. Hotel workers have to take their holidays when the hotel occupancy is less, not right in the summer. Young people want to go to the beach with their friends and to parties in July. So now it is difficult to get good staff and you have to treat them a little better to entice them and get them to stay.

(Tony Alvarez, Director,
Hotel Beatriz Palace, Fuengirola, Spain)

The same issue is seen in Dallas, Texas. Dallas is a large city. Within the city there is a high level of education among the employee base which has raised expectations and opened up many employment opportunities. Along with this a high demand for employees has reduced unemployment generally. Operating a hotel with its high staff requirements in such an environment is very challenging.

What is your main employment issue?

One of the challenges we find here in Dallas is perhaps the quality of labor that we would like to have in some of our areas such as stewarding or housekeeping and a shortage of suitable employees. For these areas employees do not necessarily have to be well educated, but they do have to be extremely hard workers. Everyone has to have a green card to have permission to work here. One of the ways we can alleviate the labor needs is to go outside the Dallas area and get our staff from other labor forces. We, in past years, as well as this year have requested help and have been granted it by the Jamaican government whereby we use Jamaican employees as well as even Romanian employees for ten months of the year. The law requires that they go home for two months of the year, and then some of them come back after our slow season (the summer) and then help us out for our fall and the rest of the year. It is an incredible resource for the hospitality industry in Dallas because they speak English. We are not the only hotel who utilizes these resources. It is a great way for the hotel to also teach these people about the hospitality business. They are here obviously for the money, but also to meet people and for the experience. We have found it to be a win/win situation for especially the Jamaican team, and we have had the Romanian team also for a couple of years and that has worked out well.

(Linda Wan, General Manager,
Hotel Crescent Court, Dallas)

In Shenzhen, China, the same problem exists with a similar solution. Situated just over the border from Hong Kong, Shenzhen has experienced huge growth in the past fifteen years. With the changes that took place when Hong Kong reverted to Chinese rule in 1997, Shenzhen has developed as a special economic zone, with a special legal status. There are many human resource challenges facing China's hotel and tourism industry, not the least of which is the lack of staff qualified to fill the roles at both operational and managerial levels. In addition, there are high staff turnover rates, coupled with an unwillingness of university graduates to enter the industry. This is also influenced by a gap between what is being taught in school and college and the realities of the industry today (Zhang & Wu, 2004). Shenzhen hotels find it difficult to get employees and recruit from rural areas of North China.

How do you deal with the staff shortages in Shenzhen?

We recruit a number of employees from northern China. To do that we go more to the poorer areas, because they are dreaming about Shenzhen as being the richest city in China—GDP wise it is—and we bring them here and mold them. They have never seen a hotel, never lived in that environment. We feel that they stay longer than the staff that are used to working in other hotels in other cities. They are more devoted. They really appreciate what we do for them—we change their life. In another ten days we will get about another fifty students coming from northeastern China. When I welcome them I say this is not just a job, your life will change totally, it will never go back to what it was. They come from little villages where there is nothing, they earn much more money than they ever could at home and their whole life changes. When they go back to their villages they have a real economic and social impact upon those villages.

(Peter Pollmeier, General Manager,
Crowne Plaza, Shenzhen, China)

Employees' expectations cause problems for management. The most significant of these is the lack of perception of what a hotel is about and guest expectations of service quality; sometimes employees are unaware of what are considered to be basic levels of service expectation. These approaches also require a very high level of commitment on the part of the hotel. The employees, coming from such a different home environment, need intense training and supervision to attain the standard required by the hotel. Because they are out of their own environment, the hotel must provide accommodation and basic needs for them—in fact, the hotel almost becomes their family.

These trends of higher levels of education and reluctance to be employed to carry out duties which are perceived to be menial tasks will continue into the future. Therefore it is necessary for hotel management to develop ways for employment within the hotel industry to be seen as more desirable, particularly by young people. Techniques and methods for accomplishing this are discussed later in this chapter.

HUMAN RESOURCES AND OCCUPANCY

The objective of a hotel is to sell the space they have and from that generate income to satisfy the investment in the property. Other operational facilities also need to be sold, and the people who work in the hotel are an essential part of that process.

There are managers who follow a "warm body" syndrome (as long as a person is alive, they are employable). However this attitude has an impact on both internal and external customers (Simons & Hinkin, 2001).

You recently only employed a small number of people out of 300 applicants?

It is hard but we cannot accept mediocrity and we don't want to get the wrong person in, so we have to stick to what we believe in. Because only 4 or 5 out of 300 were chosen, that means that only those few had the talents that we are looking for—we won't accept less. We must think long term—we can't just accept anybody. Choosing wisely eliminates the long-term negative consequences.

(Lynette Lesslar, Director, Training & Development,
Ritz-Carlton Millenia, Singapore)

What do you look for in staff?

For us it is very clear, it is not about quantity, it is about quality. If you have a good talented employee that provides quality in his work, he will perform at the level of even three bad employees. The other thing is that we require much more from employees. Most hotels just go on the technical check-in, check-out, eight hours your job has ended. Here at Ritz-Carlton it is different, you get involved. As a line employee you get involved with everything. We tell employees: you have a problem, you fix it.

(Estelita Sebeta, Executive Assistant Manager, Rooms Division,
Ritz-Carlton Millenia, Singapore)

The style, location, and type of property plus numerous other factors influence staffing requirements. Internationally there is a wide variance in the number of staff to guest ratio, as illustrated from the following comments:

What ratio of staff to guests do you operate under?

We are about one for one. At some times we go a little over that. Where the ratio is more is usually in the food and beverage area: waiters and barmen. I think at this end of the market, people like to see a lot of people about. They need to know there is someone keeping an eye on them, looking after them, without being intrusive.

(Terry Holmes, Executive Director,
The Stafford, London)

What experience have you had in relation to staff guest ratios?

Here we are very fortunate and we are running just less than one staff for each guest. In Malaysia it was higher than that: two staff to one guest and in Thailand in the Banyan Tree that I was with, because of the luxury stature of the hotel, we had four to one ratio.

(Abid Butt, Managing Director,
Turtle Bay Resort, Hawaii)

These examples represent the ratios in the hotel overall, but certain outlets in a hotel have higher and lower staff requirements. As well as having a numerical correlation between the number of guests and staff, often a cost formula is used to express this relationship. This involves a ratio of labor cost to revenue. For example, when looking at staff for a restaurant, a commonly quoted ratio is that of one-third labor cost, one-third food cost, and one-third other costs, including profit. However, when we look at actual hotels, the situation varies.

How do you deal with labor costs?

Our food and beverage labor cost percentage is about 60 percent. It is a huge challenge. I was just with the manager of this restaurant discussing this issue: about how we balance, and if there is an optimum way to do this so we don't compromise on service delivery but maximize the productivity. I don't think there is a canned formula that can be applied in all situations and at all times. From a historical perspective you learn and you develop some data and statistics, and apply it to the future and hope it works out.

(Abid Butt, Managing Director,
Turtle Bay Resort, Hawaii)

The number of employees varies widely but the challenge for management is that the ratio of employees to guests has an influence on the level of service that can be provided and also indirectly and directly on the occupancy (and therefore the profitability) of a hotel.

The employees of a hotel have an important influence on whether or not a guest chooses a particular hotel, and this can be attributed to a great extent to guest satisfaction. Barsky and Labagh (1992) conducted research in San Francisco which involved the distribution of questionnaires to hotel guests. Of the 100 guests who returned the questionnaire forty were repeat guests. Employee attitudes (service quality) was rated as the most important factor affecting hotel satisfaction. As part of the same survey (Barsky & Labagh, 1992), the guests were also asked what factors would affect their decision to not return to the hotel. The four highest-rated factors were: (1) reception, (2) service, (3) parking, and (4) employee attitudes. When the service quality and effort staff put into their jobs is recognized by management it encourages employee pride in the hotel.

What techniques do you have for recognizing staff who provide quality service?

We have ways of recognizing the job that our employees do. We have things such as our "Wow" pin where when groups come in we encourage them to give us the name(s) of staff who impressed them the most during their stay, those who did the most for them. Everyone on staff wants to win a Wow pin.

(Steve Pagano, General Manager,
Marriott Hotel, San Diego)

The recognition of employee efforts may have the effect of motivating them and thus improving the quality of service provided, however the techniques used need to be considered carefully as approaches used in one country or culture successfully may not be appropriate in another environment. Careful consideration of the programs used needs to recognize the level of the employee and that it does in fact motivate. The way a staff member feels about his or her job affects his or her performance.

In what way do you think employee satisfaction is important to what staff do?

I remember walking along in the hotel and when I asked an approaching staff member, "How are you?" The staff member answered, "Not too bad." So I stopped and asked, "What do you mean, not too bad?" She said, "I am ok." I told her, "Why don't you say 'I am having a great day' because 'Not too bad' means to me you are on defence." So I went to management and said that "Not too bad" is not acceptable in this hotel: I want the employees to tell me that they are really happy, and if they are not, to tell me why. In the results of a later employee satisfaction survey, we achieved a 96 percent employee satisfaction in the hotel.

(Octavio Gamarra, General Manager,
Ritz-Carlton Millenia, Singapore)

An employee's job satisfaction has a direct influence on the way he or she carries out duties and their willingness to provide quality service for the guest. Guest satisfaction is defined as the post-purchase evaluation of a product or service (Hum, 1977). The basic objective of satisfying customers is to improve profitability by expanding the business and, in the case of hotels, to improve occupancy (Barsky & Labagh, 1992). Customer satisfaction has a close relationship to service quality in a service environment where interpersonal relationships dominate many customer-oriented processes. Consumers form expectations, which act as a standard against which performance will be judged. A comparison of expectations and perceptions will result in either confirmation or disconfirmation (Ruyter & Bloemer, 1999). Customers' expectations are confirmed when product or service perceptions meet expectations exactly. Disconfirmation will be the result of discrepancy between expectations and perceptions. Satisfaction can be perceived in terms of a single occurrence and as an aggregated impression of a number of events. This is a critical feature for service providers (Oliver, 1996).

· Satisfied customers will be more likely to return. The relationship between satisfaction and loyalty has been observed in several studies. Fornell (1992) examined twenty-seven different businesses and found strong correlations between satisfaction and loyalty. Highly satisfied customers are much more loyal than satisfied customers. Nightingale (1985) contends that customer satisfaction leads to loyalty. Research by Jones (1990) has shown that any drop in total satisfaction results in a major drop in loyalty. Kandampully (1998) suggests that customer loyalty can be increased by ensuring that the "service promise" is maintained. In this way, the organization shows loyalty to the customer and the customer shows loyalty to the organization (Kandampully, 1998). There is a relationship between the occupancy of a hotel and maintaining guest satisfaction. If a hotel has a declining room occupancy, it can have an impact on quality of service as well as the ability to pay for quality employees.

Do you see any relationship between occupancy and human resources?

There is a dangerous situation here [in Spain] because when the hotels begin to lose their high occupancy rate, they will have to get rid of some of their employees and some of their very highly qualified employees will be the first to go. The best employees would not feel happy in a hotel which is losing its standards so the hotel would be losing one of its major assets—very high quality human resources.

(Rafael de la Fuente, Director General,
Excuela De Hosteleria, Malaga, Spain)

As has been illustrated, there is a relationship between a hotel's human resources and its guest satisfaction. An area which has for many years influenced this relationship is that of employee recruitment and turnover, and its impact on customer satisfaction and loyalty.

STAFF RECRUITMENT AND TURNOVER

The high levels of staff turnover in parts of the world is very concerning.

What is the level of staff turnover at your hotel and in Singapore generally?

Our turnover in Singapore is high. Industry-wide world-wide staff turnover for luxury hotels is about 40 percent per year. In this particular hotel it is about 30 percent which is high for our system.

(Octavia Gamarra, General Manager,
Ritz-Carlton Millenia, Singapore)

When large numbers of a hotel's employees leave in any one year it can become very costly, but although many managers identify staff turnover as a problem it is difficult to develop specific turnover-cost figures. Because of this, the bottom-line impact is not always recognized (Simons & Hinkin, 2001). The United States Department of Labor has estimated that it costs a company about one-third of a new hire's annual salary to replace a lost employee (Tanke, 2001). This includes the direct costs of replacement such as advertising, clerical time to process the paperwork, managerial time to interview, and so on, along with orientation and training.

As an attempt to quantify the costs involved in relationship to staff turnover, analysis of the costs involved was undertaken by Hinkin and Tracey (2000). As part of this research they considered the position of front-office staff. They indicated that this position was chosen because "the front-office staff in most full-service hotels comprises a large number of people, and turnover is frequently high" (Hinkin & Tracey, 2000, p. 19). For the analysis they compared the costs among four properties, two in Miami and two in New York.

There were a number of things that "had to take into account the fact that some of the human resource functions were shared between the hotels, particularly the exit interviews, recruiting, and preliminary employee screening" (Hinkin & Tracey, 2000, p. 19). The major difference between Miami and New York related to variation in the salaries paid in the two cities. The turnover cost for the first Miami Hotel was $5,965.06, for the second hotel in Miami it was $5,688.03, while New York turnover cost in the first hotel was $11,608.70, and for the second it was $12,881.65. Note that while the costs quoted in this research relate to the year 2000, it does give a tangible indication of the costs of staff turnover.

Staff turnover, perhaps more than any other factor, seems to contribute to a reduction in service quality and a sense of burnout, particularly for front-line supervisors who are constantly involved in "fire-fighting" when their departments are staffed with inexperienced employees. The position of front-line supervisor may be the most important one in the entire hotel operation, but by far the most commonly mentioned reason for line-level voluntary turnover over during the past two decades has been poor supervision. Hotels have an opportunity to gain competitive advantage by solidifying supervisors' retention and development, and the addition of incentive programs, which research has shown has the potential to significantly reduce employee turnover (Stolz, 1993).

EMPLOYEE TRAINING

Well-trained staff can build customer loyalty, which positively affects participation and boosts sales (Schechter, 1994). As part of the staff-guest relationship hotels undertake staff training programs to improve the relationship between the guest and the staff with whom they interact. Gundersen, Heide, and Olsson (1996, p. 73) state that "although there is ample literature on total quality and quality processes, few empirical studies give recommendations that can help management identify the key areas of importance to the customer."

It is therefore difficult for management within hotels to know what the guests consider to be important when evaluating the hotel experience. To improve the service, hotels use many techniques:

Do you have special training programs to help with staff quality service?

Our guest return rate is very high. Once they come here they are recognized by name and they feel at home. There is an incredibly high guest recognition factor. In our training arm we highlight and emphasize the importance of recognition. It is important for staff to use the right amount of "saying a guest's name"—you can overuse it and underuse it, and it must be just right. We use our computers for visual identification of guests. We could have ten pictures of guests coming in: Staff and concierge have access to the images so from the minute the guest sets foot in the hotel, they are recognized.

(Christopher Norton, General Manager,
Four Seasons, Singapore)

A number of models have been developed which help to explain the relationship between expectation and satisfaction. Research conducted by Boulding, Kalra, Staelin, and Zeithaml (1993) proposes a model that gives greater clarity to this relationship. At the core of the model is the assumption that "current perceptions of the service quality of a firm just after a service contact are a blend of (1) prior guest expectations of what will and should transpire during the contact and (2) the actual delivered service during the service encounter."

An alternative model by Barsky and Labagh (1992, p. 32) is demonstrated in Equation 3.1.

$$S = [(EM_1)(I_1)] + [(EM_2)(I_2)] + \cdots + [(EM_n)(I_n)] \quad (3.1)$$

where

S = Customer Satisfaction
EM = Expectations Met
I = Importance
N = Number of events

Equation 3.1 expresses customer satisfaction as a product of whether the customer's expectations are met, and how important the customer views that component of the service. This gives an overall satisfaction, which is an accumulation of a number of individual service events. The ability of managers to understand the various events which satisfy guests indicates which areas to target for training.

Training should be differentiated from orientation. Many hotels run orientation programs for their new staff; these have the objective of giving basic information to employees and are quite different from training, which seeks to increase the skills of the employee. The ability to delight a guest cannot be considered as purely a natural characteristic of the individual employee although it certainly helps reduce training. In recruitment it must be remembered that not all people are the same and not all people are suited to employment in a hotel. Note the following example:

> *Is everyone suited to employment within a hotel?*
>
> Sometimes there are people who get into the industry who are not really suited for it. I will give you a small story of this: I had a steward working with me in the restaurant and he was always under fire. He did things wrong. One day I found that he was missing. He went away for two hours and the restaurant was busy. Later when he came back I asked where he was. He replied: "I must tell you honestly—my girlfriend was sitting in the restaurant, she came with her mother, and I didn't want her to know I was working as a steward. I am sorry." So he resigned and was gone from our employment.
>
> Four years later I see a gentleman sitting in the coffee shop in an army uniform, the same man. I asked, "What are you doing here?" He said, "Sir, after I left I joined the army and I have got an award from the army. I was training as a paratrooper and I did a few jumps. My instructor was with me and he was telling me how to jump and he fell out of the aircraft without the parachute. My parachute was on and I jumped and I managed to grab him and we landed on the ground safely and he was all right." This is amazing: a man who was not fit to work as a steward becomes a hero in the army. Today (fifteen years later) he must be a major somewhere. At times you do find that—people join the industry, they realize they are not ready for it but they could do well in another field.
>
> (Vijay Wanchoo, General Manager, Corporate Planning,
> Fortune Park Hotels, New Delhi, India)

With the continued increase in the expectation for quality service by guests, the requirements for training are constantly growing and changing. Training can be conducted at a number of different levels, making training an ongoing activity.

How often do you train?

We have to continuously train our people and they have to be aware of what is happening in the world. We keep upgrading our services, keep upgrading our guest values. These are the challenges that I think are most important. They are all human related. We have a mission statement on the wall. We have our organization's practice and belief statements around the hotel and staff are encouraged to be aware of them. We directly and sometimes indirectly go through this with staff, sometimes creating a Human Resource Department intervention which leads them to the objective. This works well.

(S. M. Amzat, Senior Vice President of Operations,
Jaypee Palace Hotel, Agra, India)

How do you handle training for the inexperienced staff?

We have the philosophy and guidelines which we go through, also I came up with a lot of cross training structures for the people brought in from out of town. When they first come on board, I have a buddy system working with them. We do daily training, I do daily briefing emphasizing the basic points. There are sixteen Basics which I work through. When they are finished, we start again. You have to "preach."

(David Lim, Executive Assistant Manager F&B,
Crowne Plaza, Shenzhen, China)

To initiate a training program, it is necessary to have an outline of the topics to be covered based on the needs of your human resource. Once the needs have been identified the training course can then be specifically designed to fulfill the requirements. The process for the development, delivery, and evaluation of a training program is illustrated in Figure 3.1.

In various parts of the world, governments become directly involved in training, specifying a training levy or tax to be paid to encourage training. This approach has been used and rejected at various times, for example in the United Kingdom, a system operating in the 1960s although theoretically designed to increase the quality of training, it was subject to abuses. A current example of this type of system follows:

How do you handle the quality of staff relative to the cost of training?

To balance this it is difficult to equate. In Malaysia it is mandatory for you to contribute 1 percent to a HR development fund held by the government. It is based upon total payroll of the hotel. This amount is kept in a special fund to assist organizations for HR development. You can use this fund to reimburse your training costs. We maximize the use of this money for training—internal training (I have a good qualified training manager here) and also for external training. If you don't use it, it is gone. The cost of the training must be approved. You cannot claim 100 percent. Based on various costs, you have to submit and apply. You utilize about 80 percent over one year, so 20 percent is carried forward for the coming year. For every new associate we have, there will be an orientation course, to get them familiar with the organization, the set up, the house rules, and so on. Then we train to levels of supervision. Our emphasis is more on courtesy and I am ashamed to say that. Number one we say the customer is always right. If the customer is wrong, then we go back to number one.

(Nash Nasihin Ali, General Manager,
Mutiara Hotel, Johor, Malaysia)

If the training is to be effective it must meet the goals of the organization, it needs to be relevant to the job and it must give the trainee new skills, knowledge, or changed attitudes. In many situations not

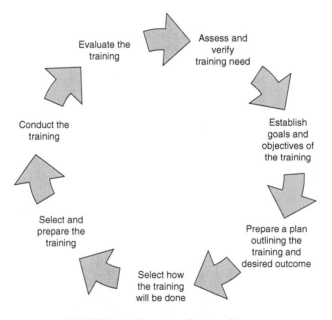

FIGURE 3.1. Steps in a Training Program

only is training given for these reasons, there is also a productivity increase requirement. It may be sufficient to measure training success in more abstract terms, but measuring in absolutes, although sometimes difficult, is important. A useful formula for this calculation is:

$$\frac{\text{Cost of training program}}{\text{Employees annual hours worked} \times \text{Rate of pay per hour}}$$

The result of this calculation is a productivity increase that would make the training a financial success along with its other objectives. The problem is that the resulting productivity change is often very small—2 or 3 percent for many training programs, and the resulting productivity is hard to measure, especially in the areas of housekeeping, restaurants, and so on.

What sort of training programs have you considered?

I had the idea of arranging training for my staff. I decided I would send my boys for fifteen days training to improve their standards. I would pay for it—it is expensive (for a suitable program they charge Rs. 10,000 per person [approximately US$227]). However, the result of that would be that those who had received the training would probably get employment elsewhere and they would leave and the benefit would go to my competition.

(P. S. Ramdas, Managing Director,
Tourist Home [Pvt.] Ltd, Egmore, Chennai, India)

EMPLOYER EXPECTATIONS

Throughout the interviews it was clear that, almost universally, the employees of hotels were recognized as the major asset of the business. Employment of people in hotel management is influenced by numerous factors such as internal constraints, industry-specific drivers, and external economy-wide factors which have a direct impact on the availability of employees and the cost of such employees (Wong, 2004). Many hotel objectives recognize the importance of the employee with most having documents which specifically detail the service and human resource relationship. Some of the hotels make sure that all members of the staff have a small, easy-to-carry reference document containing the mission statement and service goals, which they must carry while on duty. Each member of the staff has the details of what is required constantly with him or her—this gives clear focus to the ongoing training within the hotel.

It was of particular interest in the interviews the way in which different hotels and hotel groups referred to their human resource. For example the Ritz-Carlton hotel group refers to their employees as "Ladies and Gentlemen."

I understand you have a special way of referring to your staff?

At Ritz-Carlton, employees know that they are not servants, but rather ladies and gentlemen serving ladies and gentlemen. "Ladies and Gentlemen" is really a platform of how we treat each other. You put yourself on par with the guest, you are a service professional, you feel good about what you do. Our document says that our ladies and gentlemen are the greatest resource in our service commitment to our customers. This really means you feel that as an employee you are the reason why this hotel is going to be successful. . . . When you ask people what makes a great hotel, the majority say it is the service.

(Octavio Gamarra, General Manager,
Ritz-Carlton Millenia, Singapore)

The Marriott group takes a slightly different approach and refers to their employees as "Associates." While at first thought the use of these phrases may seem insignificant, there is clearly a deeper fundamental purpose to their use.

Have you always had special ways of treating your staff?

From the time when Marriott opened up their first root beer stand, it has always been in our culture to take care of our associates and our associates will take care of our guests.

Our priority is, how can we recognize our associates more often, how can we focus on developing leadership? A lot of the things we do for associates cost a lot of money.

We make sure that we talk to our associates during the day about the Basics. We do a survey every year with the associates to see how happy they are in their job that shows satisfaction levels in different areas of their work. We try and always focus on top-line sales and after that the next priority is maximizing house profit and flow through by controlling our expenses. So you are continually doing a balancing act between guest experience, associates, and profitability.

(Steve Pagano, Hotel Manager,
Marriott Hotel, San Diego)

Although the way in which employees are referred to may seem a small issue and in some parts of the world may be considered to be of little importance, the management that practices this approach reported an important change in the attitudes among employees in the hotel. A key issue when considering human resource in the hotel industry is the twenty-four hours seven-days-a-week nature of many of the positions resulting in unsociable hours, which impacts staff lives, their families, and their choice of career.

THE WORK WEEK

A key issue in all the interviews related to human resources was a shortage of motivated employees. With the change in modern attitudes, this becomes more of a challenge.

How does the work week impact your human resources?

Nowadays no-one wants to work in the hotel industry because it is nice for young people to work from nine to five and have Saturday and Sunday off. In a hotel, you must work Saturday Sunday. You have to take your holidays when the hotel occupancy is less, not right in the summer. Young people want to go to the beach, with their friends and to parties in July. So now it is difficult to get good staff.

(Toni Alvarez, Director,
Hotel Beatriz Palace, Fuengirola, Spain)

The issue of the work week is a major one, particularly as employee expectations and level of education change. Within the hotel industry there has been an expectation that employees will work six or seven days a week, but changes are taking place, for example, in Hong Kong at the JW Marriott. The Marriott group has a principle of employment that relates work hours and free time, and their employees normally work five days a week. This produces a balance between work and family. The five days are sometimes longer than normal, but it does give employees time off. In the highly competitive market in Hong Kong this approach is quite unique as the expectation of employees in the hotel industry is for a much longer employment week and so this philosophy separates the Marriott hotel from its competitors. In fact, these policies do not just impact the specific hotel, they also change the whole employment environment and can effect a social change within the employee base (Cho & Wong, 2001) which in time can impact all the properties in the market. From a broader view, reference needs to be made between the costs and benefits of such actions, the impact on the employment market and the profitability of the property.

For those in senior salaried positions in hotel employment there is a requirement for a greater commitment to the hotel:

> *What is the structure of a normal day for you?*
>
> I usually get up at five in the morning. I am at the hotel at around 5:15, dressed in my gym gear. I go to my office 5:15 to about 6:15, I do emails and prioritize my phone calls, go through the "in box" and then I am ready for the day, so I can take off. I work out at the gym until 7:15. Back to my house at 7:30, grab my breakfast, take a shower, and back to the hotel by 8:15 and then the day really begins. I try to leave 7 to 7:30 or 8 in the evening.
>
> (Christopher Norton, General Manager,
> Four Seasons, Singapore)

A senior management position in a large and successful hotel is a considerable responsibility. In such a position the manager has a huge commitment to his/her employment. Often this position takes so much time and effort it is a large drain on a person's family and outside of work lifestyle. The work expectation of employees globally outside the hotel industry is for reduced working hours, more sociable working conditions, and increased salaries. Because of the long work week within hotels workers are at a disadvantage when compared with many other industries, making recruitment and maintaining of staff more of a challenge. Managers need to find innovative ways to keep the industry seen as an attractive career option.

JOB ROTATION

Job rotation describes the practice of rotating an individual from one job to another. The aim of rotating staff is to increase the motivation of the employee by providing new experiences and challenges and giving them the opportunity to learn new skills. Critics of job rotation suggest that it is simply nothing more than instead of one person doing one boring job they do two boring jobs (Ivancevich, Olekalns, & Matteson, 1997). However, staff may be rotated within service operations when the workload is not only boring, but repetitive, strenuous, unpleasant, or costed at a different rate (Jones & Jowett, 1998).

Are you using job rotation?

Currently because of the low wages we have a lot of people doing just one job. But things are changing—we are trying to have multiskilled employment to make possible the rotation of staff. Management is trying to develop that culture; slowly we are doing it.

(S. Amarendran, Chief Executive Officer,
Breeze Hotel Ltd, Chennai, India)

The periods of rotation may be at fixed or irregular intervals and tasks can be similar or dissimilar in nature. Also the worker may make the change voluntarily, by arrangement with other workers or at the direction of management (Johnson, 1998). Certainly increasing the skill base of employees can give more flexibility to the workforce where workers can fill positions of absentees or give assistance when there are increased short term needs.

The basic requirement of an employee who is doing more than one job is that they are trained to a suitable level to be able to perform all tasks. The possibility of employees doing this depends to a large extent on the diversity of the jobs required to be completed. In the example below, the skill sets for working in the front office and working in food and beverage are quite diverse in that even though each has direct customer contact, the knowledge and skill levels are different.

How have you used job rotation in your property?

We tried to rotate the staff so that front office workers moved into food and beverage but somehow it did not work that well, unless it was just for a short time cover. Although they did get a somewhat different perspective of the jobs that others do, they had different skills.

(Vijay Wanchoo, General Manager Corporate Planning,
Fortune Park Hotels, New Delhi, India)

An important objective of rotation is to enhance the job for the employee by giving variety and changing the working environment. Rotation also has the benefit of building a multiskilled workforce. Employee agreement is necessary in the planning and implementation of rotation schemes and a major key here is consultation with all those involved.

SUMMARY

It is evident that there is a close interrelationship between the employees in a hotel and the satisfaction that a guest receives. As a result, the employees are the most important asset of the hotel. This chapter has discussed a number of key issues and ways in which employment is changing in hotels. One of these key issues, in a changing world, is to be able to recruit people who have the right characteristics for the industry. This is influenced by family perception of the industry, other opportunities for employment and increased levels of education, and expectation.

To maintain quality and standards hotel managers are constantly involved in providing training for their employees. For this to be successful the true needs of training need to be identified. The outcomes of the training need to be measured so that further requirements can be identified and met. The cost of this training is very high and therefore issues such as productivity gains need to be considered.

This chapter has also discussed the working requirements of employment in the hotel industry and the way in which employees are referred to within the organization. The importance of all these issues is that they have the objective of motivating staff so that the highest possible level of service can be given, directly impacting the profitability and sustainability of the company.

The environment in which people are employed in hotels is changing. Hotel managers throughout the world are working to increase the attraction of hotel employment and apply innovative techniques to fill their staffing requirements.

DISCUSSION

A. If you were the manager of a large international hotel what impact would you anticipate in the way you refer to your staff?

B. How could you use job rotation to enhance employee satisfaction? What negatives can you identify to job rotation?

C. You are the general manager of a large international hotel. Your human resource manager reports that it is very difficult to recruit the right type of staff. What action could you take to improve the situation?

D. You are running a hotel in a central city area. All your competitors have their staff work six or seven days a week, but you want to reduce to five days a week. What issues do you see you need to deal with?

E. You may currently or at some time have worked on a part-time basis in a hotel. Evaluate your experience in relation to commitment to the establishment where you worked. How do you think your experience would influence your management style?

F. Visit a local hotel and investigate the major human resource problems they experience and compare them to examples in this chapter.

G. If you were the general manager of a large hotel where you were having difficulty recruiting employees and you were considering recruiting from another country, what issues would you anticipate would influence your decision?

CASE STUDIES

Case Study 3.1. Engaging Staff

When you hire employees, a lot of people hire them for their hands—they just need a pair of hands to get things done. In some cases you have to hire people for their minds. My approach is not only do you hire people for their hands and their head, you hire them for their heart. If they will put their heart into their job, then you are going to have happy customers and happy shareholders and owners. We try to offer heart-felt hospitality. We have no manuals here—that is different with this hotel—there are no "procedures." I do not use the word "policies and procedures"—I have guidelines. In order to give heart-felt hospitality you need to have the employee think for themselves and do what is best for the guest and for the hotel. To do that you don't need to have them think with their head or their hands, you need them to think with their heart. If people see that we are really sincere and genuine and we are really talking and acting from the heart, it makes a big difference in how guests perceive us.

Bruce Fery, General Manager,
Grand America, Salt Lake City

Questions

1. As illustrated, the Grand America hotel has no manuals or procedures—evaluate the advantages and disadvantages of this in relationship to staff motivation.
2. Evaluate two or three hotels in your region against the criteria of the staff giving "heart-felt" service.
3. What are the factors that make the approach discussed in this case difficult in the operation of a very large top quality hotel?

Case Study 3.2. Temporary Staff As Opposed to Permanent

There is a growing trend in hotels for the employment of temporary staff to deal with the fluctuations in occupancy. But this approach provides management a significant challenge, because there is a different standard between permanent and temporary staff. For example if the hotel is short of regular room maids and we employ temporary staff from an agency, their standards and their work ethic is nothing like that of our permanent room maids. To work in a hotel the staff has to have a pride and satisfaction in doing what is not a particularly attractive job. Because of the attitudes of the temporary staff we find we have to have our housekeeper and her assistants check on them on a very regular basis, almost hourly, and once you have been checked on hourly there are two outcomes: one, the temporary staff leave or two, the temporary staff get it right so they don't have somebody coming around telling you what to do all the time.

As a manager there is a constant conflict between having the right number of staff by employing temporary people and trying to make do with permanent staff who in many respects do a better job.

Terry Holmes, Executive Director
The Stafford, London

Questions

1. You have a large conference booked in to your hotel, and you need to decide whether to employ another twenty temporary staff from an agency, or to try and make do with your current staff. What are the positive and negative issues in each option?

2. Investigate if hotels in your region use temporary staff. What benefits do they see from this action?
3. Find someone who has worked in a temporary position. Interview them to discover how they view working as a temporary employee.

Case Study 3.3. Promoting a Career in the Hospitality Industry

We have a department here at the Cumbria Tourist Board that is the Job Creation and Training team and they are to do four things. The first is raising the awareness of the opportunities that a career in tourism gives people (most U.K. people don't realize the real career opportunities, they think you come in as a waitress and this is where you stay), and of course it is women's work and it is shift work, and low paid, and unsocial hours. The first thing is to dispel all those myths and make people aware that after six months of being a waiter all of a sudden you are getting a promotion and you can be a middle manager before you are twenty, and you can own your own business before you are thirty. Second is to give some of our young people, and unemployed people and women returners, the skills that make it possible for them to access a career in tourism, so it is very much a training element. Third is to then work with the businesses themselves to make sure the career opportunities they are providing are good, so they don't get away with pokey little bedsits with no television and very poor working conditions, and split shifts and unsocial working hours. Operators are encouraged to have proper business plans and proper human resource practices. The final thing the department is charged with doing is overcoming the mismatch in Cumbria between the coastal area where there is high unemployment and the central area which is where the tourism and jobs are, so there is a job to be done there providing transport to get people to where the work is.

The whole scheme has produced some really good results. It is innovative; we are the only Tourist Board in the land that does it. Some of the research suggested that the reason why our local children won't go into the industry is that they will do a week's work experience while in high school, have a terrible experience, and come out saying that is the last time I will ever darken the door of a hotel. As a result of this we worked with the schools and schoolchildren to produce a work experience pack; the children have a copy and the hotel has a copy. So the hotel doesn't have to think about or work hard at it, they just implement it—it is a nice simple checklist approach. The child gets a better quality experience, a much more varied experience, and is much more inclined to want to come back. Another thing is they found out that high staff turnover was caused in part by poor quality induction so they have produced induction manuals, again a checklist approach, so you don't miss anything out and you can give a much more thorough induction—there are indications that this is having a positive effect. They have also set up middle managers networks and employers learning networks. They go into schools and talk to young people about career opportunities, they go to job center staff and career staff and they take them out of their work environment and take them into a five star hotel and show them behind the scenes and show what the jobs are really like now. This is a fantastic team, they do some wonderful stuff, in fact their team leader, Catherine Faire, won the Cumbria Young Director of the Year Award from the Institute of Directors last year.

Christine Collier, Chief Executive Officer
Cumbria Tourist Board, Cumbria, England

Questions

1. As a manager of a large international hotel in your region what associations would you promote to develop a growing quality employee pool?
2. How as a manager can you make more opportunities for true career development for your employees?
3. If the current trend of "young persons not wanting to work in hotels" continues, what do you see as the long-term result?
4. Investigate a hotel in your region that employs young persons. Discover actions they take, if any, to encourage long-term employment.

REFERENCES

Barsky, J.D., & Labagh, R. (1992). A strategy for customer satisfaction. *Cornell Hotel and Restaurant Administration Quarterly, 33*(5), 32-40.

Boulding, W., Kalra, A., Staelin, R., & Zeithaml, A. (1993). A dynamic process model of service quality: From expectations to behavioral intentions. *Journal of Marketing Research, 30*(1), 7-27.

Cho, Y.Y., & Wong, K.K.F. (2001). Determinants of hotel employment in Hong Kong. *Cornell Hotel and Restaurant Administration Quarterly, 42*(1), 50-60.

Fornell, C. (1992). A national customer satisfaction barometer: The Swedish experience. *Journal of Marketing, 56*(1), 6-21.

Guerrier, Y., & Lockwood, A. (1989). Core and peripheral employees in hotel operations. *Personnel Review, 18*(1), 9-15.

Gundersen, M.G., Heide, M., & Olsson, U.H. (1996). Hotel guest satisfaction among business travellers. *Cornell Hotel and Restaurant Administration Quarterly, 37*(2), 72-81.

Hinkin, T.R., & Tracey, J.B. (2000). The cost of turnover. *Cornell Hotel and Restaurant Administration Quarterly, 41*(3), 14-21.

Hum, S.H. (1997). Strategic hotel operations: Some lessons from strategic manufacturing. *International Journal of Contemporary Hospitality Management, 9*(4), 176-179.

Inman, C., & Enz, C. (1995). Shattering the myths of part-time worker. *Cornell Hotel and Restaurant Administration Quarterly, 36*(5), 74-77.

Ivancevich, J., Olekalns, M., & Matteson, M. (1997). *Organisational behaviour and management.* Sydney, Australia: McGraw-Hill Book Company Australia Pty Limited.

Johnson, D. (1998). *Human resource management in the tourism industry: Book 3.* New South Wales, Australia: McGraw Hill Book Company Australia Pty Ltd.

Jones, C., & Jowett, V. (1998). *Managing facilities.* Oxford, England: Butterworth-Heinemann.

Jones, J.P. (1990). The double jeopardy of sales promotions. *Harvard Business Review, 68*(5), 145-152.

Kandampully, J. (1998). Service quality to service loyalty: A relationship which goes beyond customer service. *Total Quality Management, 9*(6), 431-444.

Nightingale, M. (1985). The hospitality industry: Defining quality for a quality assurance programme—a study of perceptions. *The Service Industry Journal, 5*(1), 9-22.

Oliver, R.L. (1996). *Satisfaction. A behavioural perspective on the consumer.* New York: McGraw-Hill.

Ruyter, K., & Bloemer, J. (1999). Customer loyalty in extended service settings. *International Journal of Service Industry Management, 10*(3), 320-336.

Schechter, M. (1994). How to give the gift of hospitality: Great customer service. *Food Management, 29*(8), 64-74.

Simons, T., & Hinkin, T. (2001). The effect of employee turnover on hotel profit: A test across multiple hotels. *Cornell Hotel and Restaurant Administration Quarterly, 42*(4), 65-69.

Singh, R. (1992). Human resource management: A skeptical look. In B. Towers (Ed.), *The Handbook of Human Resource Management* (pp. 127-170). Oxford: Blackwell.

Stamper, C.L., & van Dyne, L. (2003). Organizational citizenship: A comparison between part-time and full-time service employees. *Cornell Hotel and Restaurant Administration Quarterly, 44*(1), 33-42.

Stolz, R.L. (1993). Reducing turnover through incentive programs. *Cornell Hotel and Restaurant Administration Quarterly, 34*(1), 79.

Tanke, M.L. (2001). *Human resources management for the hospitality industry.* (2nd Ed.). New York: Delmar, Thomson Learning.

Wong, K.K.F. (2004). Industry-specific and general environmental factors impacting on hotel employment. *International Journal of Contemporary Hospitality Management, (16)*4/5, 287-293.

Zhang, H.Q., & Wu, E. (2004). Human resources issues facing the hotel and travel industry in China. *International Journal of Contemporary Hospitality Management, 16*(7), 424.

Chapter 4

Empowerment

Empowerment is about achieving organizational goals; it means getting everyone involved in making a success of the business.

(Johnson & Redmond, 1998, p. xv)

CHAPTER OBJECTIVES

On completion of this chapter the reader will understand:

- the development and definition of empowerment
- the ways in which empowerment is introduced into an organization
- the benefits and problems associated with empowerment
- the impact of restricting empowerment
- the external influences on empowerment such as cultural, makeup of workforce, and staff motivation
- the techniques to encourage interemployee communication and problem solving
- the use of total quality management within an empowered organization
- the importance of service and the "moment of truth"
- the impact of different levels of empowerment
- the impact of culture on the empowerment of employees

The International Hotel Industry: Sustainable Management
© 2007 by The Haworth Press, Inc. All rights reserved.
doi:10.1300/5869_05

105

Key Word Definitions

24/7: Twenty-four hour operation for seven days a week.

autonomous: Ability to operate on one's own.

buzzword: A stylish or trendy word or phrase.

culture: The relatively specialized lifestyle of a group of people consisting of their values, beliefs, artifacts, ways of behaving, and ways of communicating.

moment of truth: A critical or decisive time on which much depends; a crucial moment.

quality circles: Groups designed to improve quality in the work place.

total quality management: A product-quality program whose objective is complete elimination of product defects.

Chapter Review

Empowerment is a buzzword used frequently in all types of business. Over the years its use has changed and developed. This chapter starts by giving an introduction and basic definition and requirements for empowerment and then goes on to put this theory into the "real world" environment, where its implementation is a lot more difficult than the theory may suggest. It takes a great deal of preparation and a lot of nerve on the part of managers to implement an empowered organization. It is also evident that empowerment is very often not used to its fullest extent and therefore members of staff are not truly empowered.

Empowerment of staff, if implemented, must be viewed more as an overall philosophy of operation of the property than as just one part of a management process. It has an impact that touches all the ways in which a hotel may function. Jones and Davies (1991, p. 212) define empowerment as "basically about pushing responsibility and decision making down the organization to those employees closest to the customer." The decision making ability of staff may not, in many situations, be appropriate, for example, not all staff want to make decisions. This can be for many reasons including the influences of a person's culture.

Empowerment is an essential component in total quality management requiring employees to work together. To accomplish this there are a number of different techniques which require training, and therefore there is a significant cost and time requirement. Effort must be put into promoting and applying such interaction. Some employees simply view empowerment as managers giving up their responsibility and moving it to them so staff can be blamed for management mistakes.

There are clear advantages and disadvantages to the use of empowerment and those in management positions need understanding of the positives and negatives in order to successfully implement it.

INTRODUCTION TO THEORY: EMPOWERMENT

Empowerment is the act of vesting substantial responsibility on the people nearest to the problem to be solved (Bell & Zemke, 1988). "Empowerment is regarded as one of the current management fashions" (Green & Macandrew, 1999, p. 258). In many respects it is best understood as a "generic term which covers a wide range of initiatives in the management of human resources" (Ashness & Lashley, 1995, p. 17) and which reflects a range of managerial intentions and concerns (Lashley, 1995). It is a process of training employees and enabling them to be able to deal with guest incidents on the spot and with good judgment—promptly, professionally, and courteously (Brymer, 1991). This involves a process of decentralizing decision making in an organization, whereby managers give more discretion and autonomy to frontline employees. It requires a fundamental change to the traditional hotel hierarchal organizational structure.

What do you think of empowerment in today's hotel industry?

Empowerment is an incredibly important action for any management team in any hotel.

(Terry Holmes, Executive Director,
The Stafford, London)

In its simplest form empowerment is about members of staff in a hotel being given the ability to make a decision. This can be as groups of employees or individually as part of the service encounter. For many years the hotel industry had a very hierarchical type of structure. In many establishments, there were multiple layers of workers, supervisors, and managers, which tended to be disempowering (Potterfield, 1999). This is still present in many areas of the industry. Along with many other changes in the 1980s and 1990s and necessitated by a need to make cost savings and to improve customer service, hotels adopted a much flatter organizational structure. As part of this change, groups of employees were put into teams and were encouraged to manage themselves to a much larger extent.

> Any business organization seeking to establish a customer orientation and create a good impression . . . must flatten the organizational pyramid—that is, eliminate the hierarchical tiers of responsibility in order to respond directly and quickly to customer needs. (Carlzon, 1989, p. 60)

Employees were empowered to make decisions and resolve their problems together, making it unnecessary for a member of staff to seek a management decision on what they should do in many situations. In recent years, organizations have identified the benefits of employee empowerment programs, in which empowered employees are able to solve customer and organizational problems promptly and professionally (Cacioppe, 1998). Empowerment can be a powerful tool for the resolution of problems thereby increasing the delight of guests (Bowen & Lawler, 1995). Employees can be motivated by being given the opportunity to make decisions.

> Empowered people are treated with respect. Their views are heeded. Their talents are used. They are treated fairly, praised for work well done and criticized constructively. They are prepared to work wholeheartedly with others in a worthwhile enterprise. (Johnson & Redmond, 1998, p. xv)

It is evident that empowerment is not a "soft option"; it requires considerable work on the part of all involved and strong nerves for managers. Although the literature indicates that empowerment can produce a number of positive outcomes, it is not for everyone in that some managers just do not have the personality to empower and like to keep as much as possible under their own control. This is not wrong, it is just another approach. Experience indicates that one of the more difficult things a manager can learn is to give power to others, and to support both the good and bad decisions that are made as a result.

Are there some people who do not want to be empowered?

We preach, especially in the guest contact areas, that you do whatever you need to do to make sure that the guest is happy. Some people will feel more comfortable in that position than others—maybe they have had a bad experience or they just don't feel comfortable.

What is the responsibility of managers in the use of empowerment?

Empowerment as a topic has been discussed for ages, and every organization seeks to do the best that it can. For people to feel empowered and do the things that need to happen, the supervisory or management staff need to support the right and/or the wrong decisions and at times that doesn't quite happen, so if someone makes a wrong decision and they are "crucified," then that decision will never be made again.

> (Abid Butt, Managing Director,
> Turtle Bay Resort, Hawaii)

Some very good managers are never able to accomplish successful empowerment and the empowerment of staff is restricted to task organization, for example rostering of staff, methods of work and strategies of service. These, however, are only the fringes of empowerment and are often easier for management to implement because there is less risk.

What is your attitude toward empowerment?

In one of our Basics it says, "Do whatever it takes to never lose a guest."

> (Eselita Sebeto, Executive Assistant Manager, Rooms Division,
> Ritz-Carlton Millenia, Singapore)

The overriding concept of empowerment is the ability to be involved in the decision processes of the hotel. For example, a guest approaches the front office of a hotel, explains that he or she is unhappy because the breakfast arrived late, and that influenced the timing for a number of important meetings the guest was due to have. What is the member of staff to do? One approach would be to apologize, leave the guest at the front desk, and go and ask the front office manager to speak to the guest. Another alternative would be to apologize and make an appropriate recompense, perhaps not charging for the breakfast and offering the guest possibly some additional concession by way of an apology. Then the situation can be raised at the next staff decision meeting and the issue as a whole discussed and resolutions recommended and implemented. This second approach, if conducted properly, has the effect that the guest is dealt with immediately and that they feel that their concern has been promptly resolved. The following story provides a humorous example related by a hotel manager where empowerment was not practiced:

> *A guest is sitting in a restaurant, the waiter brings a bowl of soup and places it in front of the guest and moves back to his station.*
> *Guest calls waiter over.*
>
> GUEST: I cannot eat my soup.
> WAITER: I am sorry, sir. *(Waiter immediately goes away, returns with head waiter.)* What is wrong, sir?
> GUEST: I cannot eat my soup.
>
> *(Head waiter and waiter go away and return with the chef.)*
>
> CHEF: What is wrong, sir?
> GUEST: I cannot eat my soup.
>
> *(Chef, head waiter, and waiter go away and return with the assistant hotel manager.)*
>
> ASSISTANT HOTEL MANAGER: What is wrong, sir?
> GUEST: I cannot eat my soup.
>
> *(Finally the Hotel General Manager arrives.)*
>
> HOTEL GENERAL MANAGER: What is wrong, sir?
> GUEST: I cannot eat my soup.
> HOTEL GENERAL MANAGER: Why is that?
> GUEST: I do not have a spoon.
>
> (Vijay Wanchoo, General Manager, Corporate Planning,
> Fortune Park Hotels, New Delhi, India)

The key issue of empowerment is to:

- improve quality in the service environment
- boost employee morale

Empowerment does not mean just one thing in the hotel industry, it can refer to a number of different management approaches, for example, quality circles, suggestion schemes, "moment of truth," autonomous work groups, and others. All of these have different methods of implementation and also a variety of outcomes for both the employee and the guest, and also differing levels of management commitment and resources (Lashley, 2001).

GROUP EMPOWERMENT

Group empowerment includes employees being involved with the decisions that influence what they do on a day-to-day basis, how they interact within the group, and how various groups interact together throughout the whole hotel. It has developed along with the flattening of the management structure within a hotel.

The techniques used to empower staff have had many names which have changed with fashion of the day (Dale Elkjaer & van der Wiele, 2001). However, fundamentally they have had the same goal, which is the encouragement of employees to make their own decisions in relation to their day-to-day working environment. Employees, often having direct interaction with guests, are more aware of the problems and solutions than anyone else may be. As a result they are ideally placed to manage their work environment.

How do you empower your staff?

I think empowerment is an incredibly important action for any management team in any hotel. I think that it is critical that employees feel comfortable making decisions and that requires the training, support, and tools and equipment provided by management, and then for management to give them the opportunity, the trust, the confidence to take care of whatever may come about, whether it is a decision, an opportunity to go above and beyond, whether it is an opportunity to compensate a guest for an unfortunate incident, or whatever. When a guest comes upon an employee, that employee needs to feel comfortable and knowledgeable enough to act accordingly. The last thing anyone wants today is to have to wait for another manager to come and make a decision. It is "one-stop-shopping" to use a cliché. People are very time-sensitive and they want answers quickly. We always tell our staff that if you do not know an answer that is ok, just inform the guest that you will get back to them, rather than give incorrect information. But if you are comfortable making the decision, then do it. If it is wrong, well, we learn from it and we move on. But I certainly believe that employees at all levels should be trained accordingly and should be able to make decisions in their area and any other area in the hotel where they feel they can implement it.

Have you ever had a situation where someone has given away more than they should have?

It is such a subjective type of situation. There are times that in my opinion a staff member has given a complimentary room for some situation that I think is pretty minor, but again I have to trust that person to have dealt with the situation in hand; they were with the guest and maybe that little situation disturbed the guest much more than I realize. If I question the decision, I don't react in any negative manner. I think we have to make employees feel comfortable, we have to guide them to making the decision that we believe would have been more appropriate. It is important to motivate them by saying how glad you are that they made a decision and that the guest is happy, then, continue with "Let me tell you how I would have handled that situation."

(Linda Wan, General Manager,
Dallas Crescent Court, Texas)

In this chapter, two approaches to employee group empowerment will be explored—quality circles and total quality management.

Quality Circles

Quality circles originated with the work of Edward Deming and were first implemented in the United States in the 1940s but most widely introduced in Japan in the 1960s. The central theme of this approach to the empowerment of employees is based on the importance of employees meeting regularly in groups to comprehensively discuss product quality. This involves the setting up of groups of employees to ask them how to improve the quality of their work, based on the notion that the best way to understand and improve a job is to ask the employees directly performing the tasks. Quality circles have been the target of some criticism. Some consider the technique "window dressing" and not fully resolving the question of empowerment (Prado, 2001).

At an operational level, quality circles involve employees in small groups who have responsibility for particular areas in a hotel, such as housekeeping, front office, and so on. Depending on the size of the hotel and the number of employees, these groups can be divided into subgroups. The group meets regularly to facilitate discussion and re-solve concerns among the group and promote communication be-tween groups (Ingle & Ingle, 1983). An example of group interaction is illustrated in Figure 4.1.

The interaction between the groups demonstrates how they work together to resolve problems. This group should be empowered to make decisions, recommend actions to be taken, and lead themselves, but very often, because of concerns about what the group is doing, management appoints a convener or someone from outside the group to monitor their actions and as a result the full potential of the group is not achieved. Although the purpose often is to improve communica-tion, motivation, and commitment to service quality (Dale & Lees, 1986), a problem experienced with quality circles is their long-term survival and commitment from both employees and management. Although there may be some initial enthusiasm, it becomes hard to maintain this over the long term, plus this approach requires a re-source commitment from managers to fund the time required for the meetings which they may not be willing to do. In addition, quality circles often become a "talk fest," and do not achieve empowerment by the employees.

What do you feel is real empowerment?

It is interesting—some years back people thought empowerment was the authority to give money away. But we found that by giving, for in-stance, a free meal, we were not solving the problems. So now we

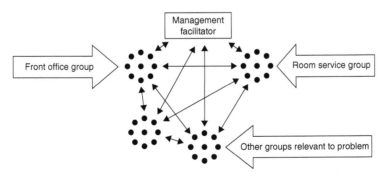

FIGURE 4.1. Quality Circle Group Interaction

have an extensive process of training. Money is the last thing to give away because there are many other ways to do it, such as offering a meal, cocktail tonight, etc. Training became part of our culture. We learned that to be empowered was actually to do things right, not just give money away. When you get empowered, you avoid giving money away and do EVERYTHING in your power to solve the problem. The key here—I use an example, the first time your father allowed you to take the car at age sixteen, he did not just give you the key and allow you to take a "killing machine" on the street, he took you through a set of rules and training. When he thought you were ready then he gave you that key. That is empowerment. When staff begin to understand this, it is easier for them to understand what it is. We empower every member of staff to do everything 100 percent correctly. That is how we use it and it works.

(Luis C. Barrios, General Manager,
Hacienda Old Town, San Diego)

Total Quality Management

The second approach is total quality management (TQM), which is a management philosophy that recognizes that the needs of the customers and the business goals are inseparable (Pike & Barnes, 1994). A central theme of TQM focuses on developing a quantitatively measured process and emphasizes the measurement of continuous quality improvement, customer involvement, and individual empowerment.

In order to successfully utilize a TQM approach, a self-confident and flexible management style is vital. It is essential that employees receive problem-solving training and have the insight to correct production problems and improve product quality. Also, employees must be able to see the product from the customer's perspective and identify flaws in quality that may cause customer dissatisfaction.

What is often missed in discussions of TQM is that it is fundamentally about the setting of standards, measuring variation from those standards, and taking corrective action. (See Chapter 5.) A commonly used example for this is:

Objective	→	Agreed Standard	→	Measurement
Reception to promptly answer the telephone.		Eighty percent of the time the phone to be answered before the third ring.		Identify variance and then action to fulfill agreed standard.

This example illustrates the point of TQM, that of determining what a standard should be and measuring variation from that standard, then taking corrective measures, which could include changing the standard or other actions that would make fulfilling the standard possible. By empowerment staff is involved in the decision process underpinned by the concept that "the person doing the job" knows best. Empowerment helps employees better prepare for their duties and how to react in the customer contact situation. A critical point of the service encounter is "the moment of truth."

MOMENT OF TRUTH

No matter the amount of preparation, with customer service there is that special moment, that decision, that response, which has the ability to delight or not delight the guest, the "moment of truth" (Carlzon, 1989, p. 3). "It is up to the top executive to become . . . devoted to creating an environment in which employees can accept and execute their responsibilities with confidence and finesse" (p. 5).

Are you satisfied with your level of service?

We won twenty-five awards last year—this is a huge number and very flattering, but we can't rest. We are only as good as the last guest served. We must keep on trying to do our best to delight customers.

(Robert Lagerwey, Assistant Hotel & F&B Manager, Ritz-Carlton Millenia, Singapore)

Although management put a lot of resources into the preparation of staff for that moment, it often comes down to exactly what decision the staff member makes at that instant of customer contact.

What are some of the ways you prepare staff for empowerment?

We have a full-time training manager on staff who does guest-type service training for the line staff. Sample questions are used and possible responses, so staff can get the idea of what they are to do and what the different options are. To a great extent this builds confidence in employees to use it on the job.

(Abid Butt, Managing Director, Turtle Bay Resort, Hawaii)

Empowerment gives employees more latitude in making on-the-spot decisions that directly affect guest service and satisfaction (Wynne, 1993), but there is clearly a balance that needs to be made between preparation, response, and flexibility. If there is too much preparation the spontaneity of the customer interaction is lost. An example that is often quoted involves stores in which the cashier says, "Have a nice day" at the end of the transaction; this is often done with no real feeling; they were told that is what they must say. In many situations this can irritate more than develop a good customer service encounter.

LEVEL OF EMPOWERMENT

The question of the level of empowerment is of importance. It is evident that some managers who say they empower their staff limit their ability to make decisions and so they are not really empowered. The following quotations from the interviews emphasize the freedom that can be given to staff:

How do you approach empowerment?

We tell staff to do what it takes—move heaven and earth to make the guest happy. We don't want the guest to leave the hotel unhappy. This is very important. Also, it doesn't always have to cost money. . . . When you calculate it, the finance versus the benefit does not compare. Benefits outweigh the cost. We don't even talk about the cost.

(Octavio Gamarra, General Manager,
Ritz-Carlton Millenia, Singapore)

Although this approach gives employees a great deal of freedom, there is considerable risk involved and management must have a great deal of confidence in staff to pursue such a policy. Many companies and managers control the ability of staff in a variety of ways. A balance of training, support, and confidence in the employees is illustrated in the following:

At what level is your staff empowered?

We give them empowerment guidelines and there is always a supervisor who has a higher level of empowerment. It is very rare that they are not able to handle the situation. In 99 percent of occasions the guest is making a request that is quite reasonable. If staff need to give a complimentary room night they can do that; if they need to reduce 50 percent off the bill, they can do that; if they need to buy the guest a room service dinner, they can do that; or maybe it is as simple as sending an apology note that the team signs. We go through extensive training sessions where we throw out every problem we can think of and provide potential solutions. They are empowered to act on their own using the solutions we have discussed.

(Steve Pagano, Hotel Manager,
Marriott Hotel & Marina, San Diego)

Many hotels provide parameters for compensating disgruntled guests.

To what level are employees empowered?

There are guidelines in writing and verbally they are briefed, and the communication tools are such that anyone is contactable any time of the day or night and instant decisions are passed. This is a dollar value depending on the situation.

(S. M. Azmat, Senior Vice President of Operations,
Jaypee Palace Hotel, Agra, India)

A number of authors have questioned whether restricting the level of empowerment given to staff actually defeats the concept of empowerment (Hales & Klidas, 1998; Reich & Copening, 1994). This can reflect a reluctance on the part of managers to give away their authority. A review of the literature reveals that a number of definitions of empowerment include that empowerment is about deciding on the boundaries of how far an employee is able to go (van Oudtshoorn & Thomas, 1995). It is suggested that restricting the level of empowerment also restricts the benefits gained through its use. Managers must try to balance empowerment and levels of responsibility:

To what level do you empower?

We have to be careful otherwise everyone can be the general manager making the final decision. We encourage "one-stop-shop" service and we encourage all the managers at contact points in their roles as managers, and not just managers, in fact anybody on the staff should have a kind of idea of how to handle situations that arise. If they are very basic rank-and-file staff they can refer to their immediate supervisor to make decisions. We have our manual and that outlines what can be done. Each level of staff has a certain power—this is what they can offer up to, but if they have to offer more than this, then they go to the next level of supervisor.

(Daisy Wong, Director, Human Resources,
Kowloon Shangri-La, Hong Kong)

The following extract illustrates how the level of empowerment is related to a particular job:

What difficulties do you get when empowering staff?

The Manager is empowered, the Senior Captains are empowered but it is not very easy today to give it to everybody down the line. They are not ready to accept it. The company policy restricts them a lot. For instance in the front office, the room discounting is very clearly defined in the policy. The General Manager can give up to 20 percent, the Front Office Manager can give 20 percent, the Receptionist can give up to 10 percent. If for some reason I have to give 40 percent I can take it to the General Manager but I cannot give 50 percent. Sometimes I have to give a room complementary, but I must justify that.

(Vijay Wanchoo, General Manager, Corporate Planning,
Fortune Park Hotels, New Delhi, India)

Staff who feel they are empowered as part of their job can assist with the quality service provided by a hotel. However, in many situations the process of empowerment gives staff additional responsibility with little or no benefits.

REWARDS AND CULTURE

The discussion of empowerment up to this point has emphasized the opportunity of staff in a hotel to become more involved in the decisions made and to feel more confident to make decisions themselves. However, many of these actions are considered to be part of the job and there is no additional reward other than self-satisfaction in the job that is being done and increased guest satisfaction; the implication is one of increased emotional labor with no reward (Wynne, 1993). As indicated by Wynne (1993), empowerment can be considered as an additional control mechanism implemented by management who use it to shift the decision accountability to the employee. When employees are empowered they become fully responsible for the decisions made. Employees who are reprimanded or criticized for making decisions that are not consistent with what their immediate senior might have done will be very reluctant to ever make a decision again. However, in the interviews there was little evidence that this was the case as all involved showed an understanding for the need to support the decisions made.

Being able to praise employees and give them a meaningful reward, allowing them to make decisions on their own, and accepting the consequences is one of the hardest things for a manager to accept (Wynne, 1993).

An additional factor influencing successful empowerment is culture. Several authors have argued that there is a relationship between empowerment and culture and this may impact the effectiveness of empowerment (Argyris, 1998; Eylon & Au, 1999; Robert Probst Martocchio et al., 2000).

The background of an employee can influence how that employee responds to empowerment. Culture does influence the way in which employees respond to empowerment opportunities; how this is dealt with is a complex question (Hui, Au, & Fock, 2004). The differing impact of the acceptance of empowerment from one country to another gives international hotel managers additional challenges and influences their success at empowerment (Hewett & Bearden, 2001; Hui, Au, & Fock, 2004).

From your experience what impact do you think culture has on empowerment?

Empowerment was a huge issue in southeast Asia, especially Thailand. It is a very hierarchical society there. They looked to the boss to make the decisions. It would have been rude for someone else to make a decision. Trying to turn that pyramid upside down would have caused difficulties.

(Abid Butt, Managing Director,
Turtle Bay Resort, Hawaii)

Do you think culture plays a part in the ability of employees to be empowered?

We have quite a diverse group of employees here at this hotel and I will say that I haven't personally experienced where the culture influenced their attitudes as much as their personality. Some people that are behind the scenes are maybe a little more introverted than those on the front desk and consequently if they come upon a situation they may not feel as comfortable expressing it or dealing with it, and I think in those situations we need to acknowledge that comfort level—in those situations you won't be able to change how people will react. However, I know that in general Asian cultures (we have two members of staff here from Indonesia) tend to be a little bit more on the reserved side until they get to know you. I think they are perhaps a little more wary and that is an opportunity that we need to identify and then we try to coach them accordingly, but for the most part I think that if we can provide them with as much knowledge as possible for making decisions, deep down inside they are capable of doing it.

(Terry Holmes, Executive Director,
The Stafford, London)

Is empowerment workable in China?

In China it is not easy. We like to say we empower staff, but if you look at rank and file staff, it is quite difficult to say, "You are allowed to make decisions worth so and so." They still feel that they need to check with the supervisor, supervisor with manager, and so on.

(Peter Pollmeier, General Manager,
Crowne Plaza, Shenzhen, China)

Is empowerment working in Malaysia?

In certain areas, yes. I do believe in empowerment but in other countries (America for instance) the word empowerment and delegation is a big thing. That culture has not been widespread in our country. There is always some form of reservation when you empower that they might be abusing the power that they are given.

(Nash Nasihin Ali, General Manager,
Mutiara Hotel, Johor, Malaysia)

LEADING AN EMPOWERED ORGANIZATION

The argument over whether empowerment is an effective tool of organizational development is not new. A review of the literature shows that organizations have a long history of trying to encourage employee participation. To this point much of the discussion has focused on the employee. Possibly to a larger extent the success or failure of empowerment is much more influenced by the senior management of the hotel. Just as some members of staff may or may not feel comfortable with empowerment, some management individuals feel the same way. Not only is it necessary to train staff to use empowerment, management also need training so they feel confident in applying its principles. It takes a lot of nerve for a manager to empower staff and to be confident that the correct practices and procedures will be carried out in relation to empowerment in an appropriate way. Clearly because of the 24/7 nature of a hotel the general manager cannot be on duty all the time and therefore must feel comfortable with what the staff is doing.

SUMMARY

This chapter has discussed some of the key issues in relation to empowerment. In theory, it may sound simple to give authority to others, but there are many concerns. Such issues as the empowerment of groups and TQM, the moment of truth, impact of culture on empowerment, and rewards have been discussed. Throughout this discussion the most critical issue is how senior management view empowerment. The way in which empowerment is implemented impacts its use, success, and failure.

Management needs to clearly understand the aims and objectives of the use of empowerment and ensure that this message is clearly conveyed to all employees. Support must be given so that staff feels comfortable in making decisions.

DISCUSSION

A. What are the characteristic differences between group empowerment and moment of truth empowerment?
B. List and discuss the characteristics in your personality that may affect your use of empowerment.
C. Identify a hotel in your locality and find out how they use empowerment.
D. What impacts do you think may result from limiting the range of empowerment?
E. What are the major advantages and disadvantages of empowerment?

F. How could you reward staff for good decision making?

G. Think of a job you have had. Were you empowered? If so what were the impacts on your employment?

CASE STUDIES

Case Study 4.1. Problem Resolution

The Ritz-Carlton Millenia Hotel is a luxury establishment strategically located with 608 guestrooms featuring unobstructed views of the Singapore skyline and Marina Bay. Stunning architecture, 25 percent larger than average guest rooms, spacious marble bathrooms, and award winning landscaped gardens featuring tropical plants, rocks, and waterfalls around the pool make very beautiful surroundings. The interior of the hotel is lavishly appointed and staff highly trained to treat their guests to the very best service that money can buy.

I started in this company as a front desk agent ten years ago. I got the opportunity to work in the hotel business, this is what I wanted to do for life. I got the opportunity to get involved and there is nothing that can engage a human being more than being part of something. If the company is successful you feel you made a contribution to that. We hire a company to survey our guests after they check out. Today we received precisely the handling of difficulties percentages where we ask the question of the guest, "Were you delighted with the problem resolution?" We got a perfect "5," that is the highest you can get. We got 100 percent. If I would have to deal with every single complaint that we have in the hotel, I would never be able to fix them all to the guests' satisfaction because there is not enough time to cope with all that. The answer is to train the employees who are dealing with the customers and they can fix the problem while they are there. We teach them to put themselves in the guest's shoes; how would you feel when you have a problem and you tell somebody about that problem—do you want to wait? No. Are you upset? Yes. Are you disappointed? Yes. Are you waiting for someone to do something? Of course. When guests say they have a problem, it is our opportunity to "step up to the plate" and fix it for them and come up with a better product. Often you have to decide are you going to do it right or are you going to exceed. Most of the time they just want things put right. Of course there are other scenarios but those are the main ones. We deal with the top 5 percent of the luxury market and those guests have special characteristics: they don't want to wait, they are all very important people. There is a VIP process in most hotels but every single guest who comes and stays here is VIP. It is extremely challenging for us to perform at that level.

(Estelita Sebeto, Executive Assistant Manager, Rooms Division, Ritz-Carlton Millenia, Singapore)

Questions

1. Why is it important for a guest to not wait for a response?
2. Think of a time when you have had need to complain about goods or services and contrast your experience with this case.
3. Is this approach applicable to only luxury hotel guests? Discuss the limitations on how this could apply in less prestigious hotels.

Case Study 4.2. 500 Years of Experience

The Sharrow Bay is a luxury country house hotel, situated on the shores of Lake Ullswater, the most northerly of the English Lakes, near Penrith, Cumbria, England. Its surrounding views of hills, lakes, and landscape are breathtaking and it has a peace and serenity which is quite unique. It is situated some eight miles from the M6 (main highway) and is described as the most sumptuous and exclusive country house hotel. Their promotional brochure states: "At Sharrow Bay you can escape to warmth, tranquility and courtesy, to an establishment whose sole purpose is the guest's comfort, where kindness and love are as important elements of the hotel keepers art as skill and experience." They state that you can "do nothing all day and feel fulfilled at the end of it, more completely human, happier in your skin."

Nick Hanson, the general manager was interviewed:

Here at Sharrow Bay we have many of the same issues that every hotel has but amplified in that the local market place is somewhat smaller. To attract a young staff the location may not appeal so we need to make sure that it is not only the awards that the hotel has won that attract the staff, we need to make sure that geographically it is going to work for them as well. We are very fortunate that we have somewhere near 500 years of experience within the staff that are here. My Restaurant manager has been here twenty-five years, chef here thirty-five years, another chef forty years, head receptionist twenty years, the housekeeper similar and I think that gives a lot of stability to the younger staff coming in. It is okay to make a commitment to somewhere—I think there are just so many opportunities worldwide particularly concerning knowledge, that after two-three years it is time to move on. The senior team here gives a lot of stability to the younger staff, there is an awful lot of knowledge here they can learn and it is about creating a family really. It is not just a job, it is about creating a whole lifestyle for them, and yes they will learn about hospitality but they can also learn about life itself. We can help them mature in their own personality. We are keen that they do go out to college and experience what else is out there. We will send them to other hotels to work in their restaurants to understand how other people approach similar problems.

This is a unique hotel. The fact that it was run by Brian and Francis for fifty years, it was their house. I think they had quite a nice philosophy that staff concentrate on looking after the guests. All the decisions were made by Brian and Francis, staff had no worries or pressures to manage, just look after the guests. My philosophy is different in that our staff are all very mature, very bright people. If they are going to make a decision, it is never going to be wildly wrong, and I just try to encourage them to embrace that. They have far more experience of Sharrow Bay than I will ever have and they are in a far better position to make a lot of the decisions.

I think everybody is concerned with consistency. You are only as good as your last meal served but I think there perhaps needs to be a higher element of risk and that will pay higher dividends. Yes, you need to empower staff but there is no joy if you don't appreciate that you have come to Sharrow Bay and it is different from staying at the Marriott—great hotels, great product for what they do. We have an opportunity here to be different and I think we need to embrace that. We would be fools not to take that opportunity. My chair, Mr. Davis, empowers me to run Sharrow Bay as if it was my own. That is a fantastic opportunity. We can nurture local suppliers. We are a focus in the local community. Sharrow Bay means an awful lot to people around here, not just the people who work here. The local community is very proud of Sharrow Bay.

(Nick Hanson, General Manager,
Sharrow Bay, Cumbria, England)

Questions

1. Sharrow Bay is an example of a small unique hotel. What empowerment issues do you see that may be different between it and an international chain hotel?
2. Investigate a small independent hotel and a hotel that is part of a large chain in your area and evaluate if there are differences in the way they empower their staff.
3. How would your management style in relation to empowerment be different if you were the manager of a small exclusive hotel from that of an international chain hotel?

REFERENCES

Argyris, C. (1998). Empowerment: The emperor's new clothes. *Harvard Business Review*, 76(3), 98-105.

Ashness, D., & Lashley, C. (1995). Empowering service workers at Harvester Restaurants. *Personnel Review*, 24(8), 17-32.

Bell, C.R., & Zemke, R. (1988). Do service procedures tie employees' hands? *Personnel Journal, September*, 76-83.

Bowen, D.E., & Lawler, E.E. (1995). Empowering service employees. *Sloan Management Review, Summer*, 73-84.

Brymer, R.A. (1991). Employee empowerment: A guest-driven leadership strategy. *Cornell Hotel and Catering Quarterly*, 32(1), 58-68.

Cacioppe, R. (1998). Structured empowerment: An award-winning program at the Burswood resort hotel. *Leadership & Organization Development Journal*, 19(5), 264-272.

Carlzon, J. (1989). *Moments of truth*. London: Harper & Row.

Dale, B.G., & Lees, J. (1986). *The development of quality circle programmes*. Sheffield England: Manpower Services Commission.

Dale, B.G., Elkjaer, M.B.F., & van der Wiele, A. (2001). Fad, fashion, and fit: An examination of quality circles, business process reengineering, and statistical process control. *International Journal of Production Economics*, 73(2), 137.

Eylon, D., & Au, K.Y. (1999). Exploring empowerment cross-cultural differences along the power distance dimension. *International Journal of Intercultural Relations*, 23, 373-385.

Green, N.D.A., & Macandrew, J. (1999). Re-empowering the empowered—The ultimate challenge? *Personnel Review*, 28(3), 258.

Hales, C., & Klidas, A. (1998). Empowerment in five-star hotels: Choice, voice, or rhetoric? *International Journal of Contemporary Hospitality Management*, 10(3), 88.

Hewett, K., & Bearden, W.O. (2001). Dependence, trust, and relational behavior on the part of foreign subsidiary marketing operations: Implications for managing global marketing operations. *Journal of Marketing*, 65, 51-66.

Hui, M.K., Au, K., & Fock, H. (2004). Empowerment effects across cultures. *Journal of International Business Studies*, 35(1), 46-60.

Ingle, S., & Ingle, N. (1983). *Quality circles in service industries*. Englewood Cliffs, NJ: Prentice-Hall, Inc.

Johnson, R., & Redmond, D. (1998). *The art of empowerment—The profit and pain of employee involvement*. London: Pitman Publishing.

Jones, P., & Davies, A. (1991). Empowerment: A study of general managers of Four-Star properties. *International Journal of Hospitality Management*, 10(3), 211-217.

Lashley, C. (1995). Towards an understanding of employee empowerment in hospitality. *International Journal of Contemporary Hospitality Management*, 7(1), 27-32.

Lashley, C. (2001). *Empowerment HR strategies for service excellence*. Oxford, England: Butterworth Heinemann.

Pike, J., & Barnes, R. (1994). *TQM in action*. London: Chapman & Hill.

Potterfield, T.A. (1999). *The business of empowerment: Democracy and ideology in the workplace*. Westport, CT: Quorum.

Prado, J.C. (2001). Beyond quality circles and improvement teams. *Total Quality Management*, 12(6), 789.

Reich, R., & Copening, L. (1994). Empowerment without the rhetoric. *Quality Progress, Jun,* 27, 25-37.

Robert, C., Probst, T.M., Martocchio, J.J., Drasgow, F., & Lawler, J.J. (2000). Empowerment and continuous improvement in the United States, Mexico, Poland and India: Predicting fit on the basis of the dimensions of power distance and individualism. *Journal of Applied Psychology*, 85, 643-658.

Van Oudtshoorn, M., & Thomas, L. (1993). A management synopsis of empower-
    ment. *Training for Quality*, 3(3), 25-27.
Wynne, J. (1993). Power relationships and empowerment in hotels. *Employee Rela-
    tions*, 15(2), 42-51.

Chapter 5

Resource Management

Time and tide wait for no man.

Proverb

CHAPTER OBJECTIVES

On completion of this chapter the reader will understand:

- the importance of physical resource management
- the management of assets in the hotel industry
- the use of standards in understanding operations related issues
- the application of variance analysis and the resulting management decisions
- the purchase of goods and services in a competitive environment
- the requirements for a secure operational environment
- the impact that hotel ownership has on operational decisions
- the life expectation of a hotel and the question of refurbishment in changing environments
- the planning of maintenance
- the influence housekeeping has on guest satisfaction and interconnectivity
- the use of outsourcing in asset management

The International Hotel Industry: Sustainable Management
© 2007 by The Haworth Press, Inc. All rights reserved.
doi:10.1300/5869_06

Key Word Definitions

assets: Items that hold commercial or exchange value.

competitive advantage: The strategies, skills, knowledge, resources, or competencies that differentiate a business from its competitors.

core competencies: Relating to a company's particular area of skill and competence that best contribute to its ability to compete.

environmental scanning: Maintaining awareness of the environment the business is operating in to use in future and current planning.

functional obsolescence: Defects in a building or structure that detract from its value or marketability.

interconnectivity: The ability of two or more to interact in a meaningful way.

SARS: Severe Acute Respiratory Syndrome.

variance analysis: The analysis of variation from a determined standard.

Chapter Review

Hotels are complex environments in which many different resources come together to satisfy the various stakeholders including the guest, the owners/investors, staff, management, and the local environment in which the hotel operates. Physical and human resources influence each of these and therefore need constant monitoring and management attention. The purpose of this chapter is to investigate the resources of a hotel and highlight areas that need particular attention. Within the hotel industry many of the assets used in the production process are difficult to control; they are subject to such issues as theft, spoilage, deterioration, as well as forms of misuse. The ability of managers to monitor the use of such assets has a direct impact on the success of a hotel. In many instances this requires the setting of standards and the correct measurement of variation from the standard. The global environment in which a hotel operates is influenced by many factors outside the control of the hotel. Issues such as security, health, economic, and social issues change the operational environment.

Senior management in a hotel needs to work with the owners of the property in an appropriate way to maximize outcomes for all parties. The ownership of hotels may come about in various ways, from institutional owners who are simply interested in the financial return to hands-on owners who become involved on a daily basis. In many respects the life expectation of a hotel and the refurbishment plan are not only directly related to the ownership of the property, but also linked to issues such as guest satisfaction, guest expectations, and the financial long-term return.

What is your objective as manager of the hotel?

There is no question that we are here to make a profit for our owners, but on a day-to-day basis we are here to look after our guests. When our guests return these sales translate into a profit for our owners.

(Steve Pagano, Hotel Manager,
Marriott Hotel, San Diego)

Within a hotel, the various departments have to work together to ensure a quality product. One of the most important of these is housekeeping. This chapter discusses the interconnectivity of this department with others, along with the growing trend of outsourcing.

INTRODUCTION TO THEORY: RESOURCE MANAGEMENT

The types of assets involved within the hotel industry, both human and nonhuman make management more difficult than many other industries. For example, in the bar there is a bottle containing a liquid that has a cost, often a certain amount needing to be measured with the resulting measured quantity being delivered to a guest. This is often mixed with other ingredients so that revenue is generated with a desired level of profit. In the kitchen a mixture of different ingredients needs to be added in the correct combination to deliver some finished product to a restaurant guest, again to obtain a desired return to the business. Along with this, hygiene and health and safety issues need careful consideration. In housekeeping there are cleaning materials which have a high cost and influence profitability; therefore they need to be controlled, and there are hazards associated with their use that need to be managed. Throughout the hotel there are staff being paid, the guests have access to facilities, and there is an investment in the hotel building (Jones, 2002). All of these assets need to be used so that an appropriate return for the business is achieved (Feldman, 1995). Vigilant managers constantly monitor each of these factors to accomplish this objective.

Maintaining costs must be a real challenge, how do you do that?

A couple of months ago I gave a manager a challenge. He happened to have a high cost of goods in his area, and I said the reason why we haven't done so well in the area is that you haven't focused enough. I know this person well enough to say, "I know that if you make this your top priority, we can fix our cost of sales." Over a couple of months we have made a dramatic change. The only reason is that person has made it a focus for himself. If you make it a priority you can be very successful.

(Bruce Fery, General Manager,
Grand America, Salt Lake City)

The challenge to all hotel managers is controlling the assets of the business while not restricting the assets to the point that quality service is inhibited. It would be possible to lock every asset up, and when required have security deliver the item, but the delays and inconvenience would outweigh any possible savings. From the interviews with the senior management in hotels it was discovered that there were issues that directly impacted the day-to-day operations and in particular the control and profit from assets that required planning and direct management action. Management is also influenced by the local conditions in which they operate.

What issues impact your control of profits?

India is a country where there is a lot of liquor imported, particularly from England, but you also get a lot that is smuggled which makes the management of liquor complicated. It is important to also know the legal requirements of selling alcohol. For example, there are three days in India where you don't sell liquor at all: January 26, August 15, and October 2. You need to make decisions accordingly. No F&B manager will break it or he goes behind bars. The rule is that in the rooms you can have it. There is an L3 license for rooms, L5 for restaurants, L20 for banqueting. On those three days L20 and L5 you cannot sell but it can be in the rooms. The understanding and knowledge is all important to plan and manage this type of restriction.

(Vijay Wanchoo, General Manager, Corporate Planning,
Fortune Park Hotels, New Delhi, India)

As discussed in Chapter 4, the staff should feel they have the ability to make decisions in relation to the hotel's assets, but these decisions need to be appropriate at the time. The key to controlling assets in the hotel industry is the setting of standards, measuring against those standards, and then taking corrective action.

STANDARDS

Kreck (1978) defined the process of understanding, setting, and measuring standards under ten clear steps:

1. Define outcomes
2. Describe the symptoms
3. Verify the symptoms
4. Discover any trends
5. Identify critical areas
6. Ascertain critical principles
7. Make comparisons
8. Develop solutions
9. Carry out testing
10. Compare results

This approach, although not new to decision making, emphasizes the importance of being able to correctly understand what the problem is; this ensures that you are actually trying to resolve the cause of the problem. This is followed by taking corrective action, and carefully measuring the outcomes to ensure that the desired results are being achieved. Once the standard is set in many cases it is simply the comparison of a standard to an actual result and evaluating the variance to formulate management decisions. The standards can be defined in many different ways:

How can you define standards?

In some of our training sessions I use an example about the person who cleans the windshield on the car. If that person's job was to clean the windshield, then your standard of cleanliness might be different to mine, as opposed to if you defined that person's job "to provide clear vision for the driver." Then all of a sudden it is a different definition. As long as the driver says it is clean, then I am done; if the driver says it is not clean, then I have to keep cleaning. That's about the only way to standardize it. Is the person occupying the room going to see the room as clean or to look at it that the room has not been cleaned properly.

(Abid Butt, Managing Director,
Turtle Bay Resort, Hawaii)

VARIANCE ANALYSIS

Jagels and Coltman (2004, pp. 219-222) specifically deals with food and beverage management. The first step involves the establishment of a standard, which in this case involves identifying the cost of the ingredients of each item in the menu. This is done with the assistance of a standard recipe that lists all the ingredients, production process, and portion sizes. Once a standard is established, it is straightforward to calculate what the total standard is by multiplying the cost of an individual menu item by the number sold. The result is the standard cost, or what total cost should be for the items sold. At the same time because each item has a different selling price the quantity of each item sold is multiplied by the number sold. This results in the standard revenue figure. Two additional pieces of information are required—first, the actual amount of ingredients used. This is produced by taking the opening inventory, adding to it purchases and subtracting the closing inventory. The second is the actual amount of cash received. This provides four pieces of information: standard cost, standard revenue, actual cost, and actual revenue, resulting in four alternatives:

1. Total Standard Cost is > than Total Actual Cost
2. Total Standard Cost is < than Total Actual Cost
3. Total Standard Revenue is > than Total Actual Revenue
4. Total Standard Revenue is < than Total Actual Revenue

The principle of comparison between standard and actual has wider application. For example, the standard use of cleaning materials by housekeeping compared to actual; the number of guest rooms cleaned in an eight-hour shift in a hotel; the number of guests served in a restaurant by one person, and so on. In any situation where a standard can be established, management can measure that standard against actual performance.

PURCHASING

The purchasing of goods and services in a hotel is an important part of the day-to-day operations. Although a hotel may have a purchasing department that takes care of the routine operations, management needs to keep a constant watch on the decisions that are being made. There are two main reasons for this, the first is that the purchases of goods and services account for a large amount of the hotel's expenditure and second, the items purchased by a hotel are subject to various issues including theft and fraud.

An important question when considering purchasing goods and services is to correctly understand the need for the purchase. The need and the person responsible for that need must be clearly identified. In many instances it may be nice to have certain ingredients in a kitchen, certain cleaning materials and equipment in the housekeeping department, and certain computerized facilities in the accounts department, but they should be purchased if only they are absolutely necessary to fulfill specific requirements. The purchasing department needs to ask itself the question: is it necessary? If so, what quality is required? Can a similar item that produces the same quality but at a lower cost be used? As the items purchased tie up money and storage space, each of these has an impact on the profitability of a hotel, and should be minimized.

There is a requirement that the goods and services meet the expectations of the guests and also are cost effective. As illustrated from the following, there are specific and changing guest expectations:

How are the changing expectations of the guests influencing hotel purchases?

The product has to be the finest; it is as simple as that. From a bedding point of view, from a technology point of view—technology has become this huge issue now. DVD players and CD players we have in our suites, customers are happy with that but now we are looking at having MP3 hookups, because people come with MP3s and they can be connected with the speakers. Constantly you have to be looking at what is out there, what is the latest technology. We are looking at MP3 TVs. It is an expensive proposition. It is very difficult for me to convince the owners about this. The guests have 42″ TVs in their home, they experience this, it is their norm. It is always a balance that you seek.

(Octavia Gamarra, General Manager,
Ritz-Carlton Millenia, Singapore)

The purchase of goods and services requires accurate record keeping and monitoring. Many of the items purchased by a hotel are small, expensive, and easily misappropriated. The best way to have control over these items is to divide the responsibility for assets among several persons. It is bad practice to have the same person order goods, receive the goods, and account for the goods. Also, job rotation helps to reduce the possibility of one particular employee defrauding the hotel and being able to cover it up. Often fraud is a long-term operation on the part of an employee; the possibility that they may at any time be moved to another position in the hotel may reduce opportunities to undertake fraudulent activity. In addition limiting access to assets is essential.

How do you balance guest expectations and hotel profit requirements?

We try and always focus on top line sales and after that the next priority is maximizing house profit and flow through by controlling our expenses. Obviously with this strategy you are continually doing a balancing act between guest experience, associate satisfaction, and profitability. On the guest side we look at guest satisfaction survey results along with verbatims every week. Based on this information we develop processes to ensure high levels of customer satisfaction and a strong desire to return. On the profit side we continually look at our largest expense which is payroll and determine the proper balance between staffing levels to assure great service, and payroll costs. The key is in staffing up when needed and reducing staffing levels when ever possible. In a large hotel this is a very complex challenge and one that a great deal of time is spent on. Improving productivity is the key.

(Steve Pagano, Hotel Manager,
Marriott Hotel & Marina, San Diego)

A sound management technique is to be unpredictable; unexpected inventory checks, be aware of what is going out in the garbage; managers need to be observant of all the operations happening within the hotel.

HEALTH AND SAFETY ISSUES

The world in which hotels operate has changed over the past few years; terrorism and international health issues have impacted the hotel business in all parts of the world.

How are world events impacting hotel operations?

The world is a complex place: terrorism, the Iraq war, then SARS, and the resulting economic downturn. A lot of travelers are very cautious: they are thinking very carefully about what they are doing; they are including these issues into their decision making processes.

(Nash Nasihin Ali, General Manager,
Mutiara Hotel, Johor, Malaysia)

Although events such as SARS, and terrorist attacks have had very significant impacts on hotels, it is also useful for management to take these events and look at the long-term situation, as suggested in the following:

How do you see world events changing the way you manage your property?

We diagnose our hotel by segmentation. Of course over 9/11 we saw a drop. The trend itself would be irregular anyway because first of all there was 9/11, the bombings and SARS. You really need to monitor what your trends are like. We look over the last eight years and that helps us forecast accurately.

(William Chu, Director, Revenue Strategy,
Ritz-Carlton Millenia, Singapore)

In addition, as a manager looks at the long-term operations of a hotel, in periods where epidemics such as SARS have an almost immediate impact on occupancy, there needs to be consideration of the human resources employed by the hotel. In this situation cooperative management is essential. Management need to have open discussions with their employees to find ways to overcome what is hoped to be a short-term event. This is important as at some time in the future occupancy levels will return and the guests will have expectations of quality service.

What action did you take when SARS had such an adverse effect on your occupancy?

At that time we sent some staff out to other properties so they can grow from the exposure. Also we were doing renovation at that time. Some took vacation. We sent a number of staff to Japan to learn and freshen up their knowledge of Japanese hospitality (chefs, waiting staff, waitresses, and assistant managers). It was really good for the staff. At that time we had quite a few hotels that were opening. Two groups of staff went to Sydney and Dubai. Staff were encouraged to clear their outstanding annual leave and then we had a voluntary unpaid leave scheme. We used the rest of the staff to keep the hotel running.

(Belinda Goh, Director, Sales & Marketing,
Shangri-La Kowloon, Hong Kong)

A particularly interesting situation was revealed during the interviews in the English Lake District. There had been an outbreak of foot and mouth disease in 2001. All species of cloven-hoofed animals are susceptible and the disease is extremely contagious. Large areas of Britain had restricted access and the outbreak almost completely destroyed tourism activities in many parts of England.

How did the Foot and Mouth outbreak affect accommodation providers?

Foot and Mouth—a devastating year for us. Some businesses did well, others didn't do well, in fact they did drastically. Those that did well were hotels which accommodated vets, scientists, the media, politicians, and everybody who came to just look and do things relating to the problem. One of the things that we learned, with tourism there are winners and losers. It doesn't matter what the situation, barring all-out nuclear war, you have winners and losers. So, tourism in a perverse way has a bit of a stabilizing influence on an economy, even during the worst of events. That was quite a useful lesson to learn.

(Christine Collier, CEO,
Cumbria Tourist Board, Cumbria, England)

Since the number of people employed in a hotel is large, health and safety is an important issue. The employees could be associated with terrorist groups or be carriers of contagious diseases. The screening of staff to be employed is an important issue.

Have security issues changed your employment processes?

Not in material terms. In certain positions we definitely go for the security checks into backgrounds, police reports, and so on the same as you would for someone who was going to handle cash, you would want to look at their credit reports. So no major changes.

(Abid Butt, Managing Director,
Turtle Bay Resort, Hawaii)

Have security issues changed the employment processes?

We do a background check of all employees. That has been a policy also in the past. We determine the family background, the education of the people.

(S. M. Azmat, Senior Vice President of Operations,
Jaypee Palace Hotel, Agra, India)

Regarding security, it was of particular note during interviews with senior management how issues such as access have changed. It was not too many years ago that a hotel was considered to be a very public area; it was not difficult to obtain access to many areas of the hotel, in particular there has been a lot of effort placed on training of staff and raising their awareness of security issues. In one of the general manager's offices that was visited there was almost a full wall of security TV monitors that were constantly changing to a variety of cameras throughout the hotel, including staff areas. During the interview there was the feeling that the general manager was constantly aware of what was on the monitors. The following illustrate a variety of approaches:

How have security concerns changed how you operate?

No real specific changes other than possibly more closed circuit security cameras installed, more awareness type training to encourage staff what to watch out for. Hopefully the industry would not get to the point of having yet another metal detector to go through to get into the hotel.

(Abid Butt, Managing Director,
Turtle Bay Resort, Hawaii)

In what ways have security issues changed the things you do?

We are much more inclined to have security people walking the parking lots. We do not search cars, but there is a presence there and guests are aware of it. We have seminars every year where we bring security people in to train with ideas of what to do when things happen, how to find suspicious people, and so on. A lot of awareness. Hotels are very easy to attack—we are aware.

(Luis C Barrios, General Manager,
Hacienda Hotel Old Town, San Diego)

Have security concerns changed what you do as a hotel?

If it was before 9/11 I don't think people were that security conscious, but now we are more aware that there could be a potential problem. We take more precautions in making sure our guests are safe both from a life safety point of view and just in general. It is on our mind more and we are more aware of it. We did not add any staff, we are just more alert.

(Bruce Fery, General Manager,
Grand America, Salt Lake City)

How do you deal with the question of security?

We certainly have a much greater awareness as to what is going on around us. We have always had the guests' best interests in mind in that we designate guest stations and public areas and we have a very good team who are trained in customer service and can certainly recognize any people who should not be on the property. In that sense we all are affected by the fact that we should always be aware of security everywhere we go. We always promote safety everywhere we go, in rooms, in public places, and in our offices and so from that perspective it is much more in the forefront of everyone's minds.

(Linda Wan, General Manager,
Hotel Crescent Court, Dallas)

An interesting recent innovation has been the ability of guests to view security cameras from their in-room televisions. For example, a guest can look at the corridor outside their room, at the car park, and other public areas. This is designed to give guests a greater feeling of security; however, it could simply make guests overly concerned with security issues.

HOTEL OWNERSHIP

In most cases, hotel ownership is entered into for financial return. The owner's perspective of a hotel may be different from that of the senior management, but for both sides to be satisfied, parties need to be able to work together to the advantage of all.

How has hotel ownership changed over the past few years?

The industry has changed a great deal, at least in the United States in the last ten years. Prior to that it was all institutional ownership, equitable insurance would have owned and the hotel was an asset [that] would have just been kept there. It wasn't their core business. But now a lot of the owners are very actively involved with what is being done with their assets.

(Abid Butt, Managing Director,
Turtle Bay Resort, Hawaii)

The involvement of the owners in the day-to-day operations can be very different from one hotel to another, as illustrated in the following, but what is also apparent is the amount of effort that management need to put into working with the property owners:

What about ownership of the hotel?

All our properties are privately owned by individuals. People from all over India. One of the difficulties is that they are not hoteliers. One may be building bodies for buses, another in the steel industry, another in the shipping industry. This makes their understanding of the hotel industry very limited.

(Vijay Wanchoo, General Manager, Corporate Planning,
Fortune Park Hotels, New Delhi, India)

How much of your time is spent with the owners of the hotel?

The owners' office is just across the street. They are great people and they are very, very involved. Sometimes they phone and say. . . . This is going on in the hotel. Something that is very different in Asia then is the involvement of the owners; 30 percent of my time is managing the owners. It is part of the duties of the general manager, not only to run the hotel but much of my time is with the owners. Often owners are families, not companies. Again great balance is required—you have to be very political when you are dealing with the owners. You have standards and you are constantly balancing.

(Octavia Gamarra, General Manager,
Ritz-Carlton Millenia, Singapore)

In addition to what may be considered as the negatives of owner involvement, it is clear that good working relations with the hotel owners also results in further investment and development of the property:

What impact do the owners have upon the way you run this hotel?

I always say that it starts with the relationship between the partners, the owners, and management company. In this case we are very lucky to work with an owner who gave us a great product. They spent a lot of money on this place and they have the same vision that we have. They want this hotel successful and are looking at it long term. Many owners have their own ideas. Here we have a strong partnership between two companies wanting the same thing.

(Peter Pollmeier, General Manager,
Crowne Plaza, Shenzhen, China)

HOTEL LIFE CYCLE

As we look at hotels internationally we see that there are a number of well-established properties that have been in existence for many years. In the first five to ten years of existence, the hotel goes through rapid growth in both occupancy and net income. After this period of growth the occupancy stabilizes and the income remains fairly constant up until the hotel is about fifteen years old (Rushmore, 1992). As indicated through research by Rushmore (1992), the total life expectancy of a hotel is approximately forty years, but this figure has a standard deviation of twenty years.

The life cycle of a hotel is also influenced by its location.

How do facilities relate to your location?

For any hotels in a tropical environment, especially those that are close to the ocean, the physical plant goes through enormous amounts of challenge. This coastal environment was possibly not meant for concrete, it was meant for thatched roofs. This building takes a massive beating from the elements. Despite the advances in modern paints, mother nature still takes its toll. Humidity in the air can even rust out the telephone jacks in the guest rooms so we are applying gel to that. It is a totally different operating environment compared to New York or Los Angeles.

(Abid Butt, Managing Director,
Turtle Bay Resort, Hawaii)

As illustrated in the case of Hawaii there are a large number of factors that influence the facilities and the useful life expectancy of a hotel (Jones & Jowett, 1998). These include loss in income and value resulting from outside factors such as declining neighborhoods and, as discussed in the chapter on yield management, poor management of the room rack rate resulting in short-term income but in the long term, insufficient reserves to maintain the quality and appearance of the property. Revenue loss stemming from out-of-date appearance and inferior facilities is functional obsolescence, and this can be key to hotel value decline (Rushmore, 1992).

How do you maintain high occupancy in relation to the quality of facilities?

A lot of the hotels particularly in Malaysia are experiencing cash flow problems and when you have a cash flow problem, you would rather sell a little bit lower so you would have enough cash turn around. The room rate is reduced to increase occupancy percentages, but the high level of occupancy causes greater deterioration of the facilities. Because the facilities are deteriorating a lower room rate is charged and so forth. The problem is that as the property declines there is insufficient revenue to maintain the facilities because of the low room rates being charged.

(Nash Nasihin Ali, General Manager,
Mutiara Hotel, Johor, Malaysia)

Many older hotels in the declining phase of their life cycles have good locations and sound structures. They are prime candidates for massive overhauls, which will add years to their lives. In other situations where the neighborhood of the property has deteriorated, management is faced with a more difficult decision on the possible future of the property considering whether it would be better changed into something else or simply demolished and completely redeveloped.

HOTEL REFURBISHMENT

With a life expectancy of about twenty to sixty years, a property goes through many changes, but at some point there is a growing need to refurbish. This can be characterized as either major or minor refurbishment that arises when

- a hotel has become uncompetitive due to outdated standards and lack of life cycle refurbishment.
- the benefits of the site, building character and known market offer the prospect of increased business (Lawson, 1995).

The sales value of a hotel is strongly influenced by the market the hotel is operating in, the life stage that it is in, and reflects the market demand and yield. The level, cost, and extent of the refurbishment carried out can vary a great deal. There is today, a higher level of expectation by guests for the facilities within a hotel.

How do expectations change the facilities you provide?

Our customer expectations continually change. I believe the rule is that our rooms have to be at least as good as what the guest has at home. Comfortable beds with feather toppers, great linens, and pillows. In the public spaces the fitness center must be as good as where they work out at home; the restaurants must be as good as their neighborhood favorite.

(Steve Pagano, Hotel Manager,
Marriott Hotel & Marina, San Diego)

Therefore, when a property is in the process of being refurbished, guest expectations in the target market must be considered. A hotel needs to maintain a competitive range of facilities that takes into consideration the future technological development during refurbishment of the hotels rooms and other facilities (Loether, 2005). This includes updating the audiovisual and telecommunications conduit, cabling, connectivity, and controls, although recent advancements in wireless technology has significantly improved the ability to add Internet and audio visual and communication facilities without having to install cables.

Is it a challenge offering the modern technology in this older, well-established type of hotel?

Yes, suddenly you are putting in the WIFI and we have had all sorts of technical problems. It is very hard to get a mobile phone signal in the Stafford—a lot of people think I do it on purpose so they have to use our phones. I had no problem with people not being able to use their mobiles but there becomes a demand for it and last year we had a very big piece of business and the chairman and the cochairman said we will never stay here again if you don't get the phone system so we can use our mobile phones and so we have spent quite a lot of money putting in boosters. In some hotels you go into a room and you almost need a PhD in science to turn on the lights. You can make a room far too complicated and far too technical but you have to keep up with things that come along. Just putting in air conditioning in a hotel like this was an enormous task. The first thing I did years ago when I knew we couldn't afford air conditioning, I put in big ceiling fans and that was quite a step forward and then when we put in air conditioning we kept the ceiling fans because not everyone likes air conditioning. It is important to keep up-to-date with what's going on, but ensuring that the "feel" continues, and that you don't turn it into something that people aren't expecting.

(Terry Holmes, Executive Director,
The Stafford, London)

As mentioned previously, the surroundings of the hotel, its location, surrounding businesses, and other developments in the vicinity influence the success of the hotel. This requires managers to be involved in environmental scanning, proactively involved in local affairs and in particular with local government committees.

How do you work with changes that occur in your surrounding area?

We wrote to the government regarding the street sleepers especially around our area. Their response was to put in some very big potted plants there to deter them. As a quality hotel we need quality facilities, and a quality area. The government has tried to make Tsim Sha Tsui more beautiful with gardens and plants. We wrote to them several times already and now they are making improvements. The government also has plans to beautify the promenade. The Kowloon Canton Railway providing train service to the border of Mainland China, along with a moving walkway, sheltered and air conditioned, linked to the Mass Transit Railway (MTR) will be in service later this year, a big improvement in the infrastructure. These changes are all important to us.

(Patsy Chan, Director of Communications,
Shangri-La Kowloon, Hong Kong)

As part of refurbishment it is also beneficial to consider if the hotel can be given a competitive advantage. The core elements of a hotel are (1) the building, its interior, and environment in which it resides, (2) the guest rooms, facilities available, and appearance, and (3) the reception and public areas of the hotel. Competitive advantage can be accomplished through many measures; it could be simply the room rate charged or the quality of service, as well as the facilities offered. Understanding guest needs and wants would guide management to be able to provide the level of facilities that would be appropriate. As illustrated, what was once considered to be a competitive advantage may not necessarily remain so.

> *What facility demands are changing your property?*
>
> Now every business traveler wants in-room Internet facility. We don't have that at the moment but soon we are signing an agreement with a supplier. We have no choice. We have to convince the owner to come up with the money because now it is expected.
>
> (Nash Nasihin Ali, General Manager,
> Mutiara Hotel, Johor, Malaysia)

MAINTENANCE PLANNING

The process of maintenance management in a hotel is often a shared responsibility, although it may be allocated directly to the maintenance department. There are many hotel general managers who spend a great deal of their time walking around the hotel noticing things that need attention.

The very inevitability of maintenance is the factor that tends to obscure its importance. Lack of maintenance can very quickly impact the appearance, efficiency, and guest satisfaction in a hotel. The ability of management to maintain a property is often closely related to the profitability of the hotel (for further discussion, see the chapter on yield management).

The three basic requirements of a planned maintenance system are

1. a program of maintenance activity for the hotel, its plant, and equipment;
2. a means of ensuring that the hotel's program of maintenance is fulfilled; and
3. a method of recording and assessing the hotel's maintenance.

As this list shows, there is a need for management to identify, plan for, and record the maintenance requirements of the hotel. This process involves all parts of the hotel, not just those areas visible to the guest, illustrated as follows:

What actions do you take to maintain constant quality in your property?

Housekeeping does inspections every day, our Customer Satisfaction Team does inspections every day and then meets with Engineering and Housekeeping every Friday to review and strategize. When we do the inspections, Housekeeping doesn't know what rooms we are going to, so they can't prep them. If I see a lot of problems then I step up the inspections. Our Perfect Room Teams go into four rooms every day and they do the deep cleaning. They have a different check list from the housekeepers. There is a team of three and they go into the room with their tasks—tub tile, floor tile, shampooing the carpet, painting furniture touch up, wallpaper vinyl repair. When the perfect room team leaves at the end of the day that room is in as perfect a shape as it can be without being completely refurbished.

(Steve Pagano, Hotel Manager,
Marriott Hotel & Marina, San Diego)

Understanding the life expectancy of items in the hotel helps with good maintenance. For example, a light bulb has an expectation of life—this can vary depending on the number of times it is switched on and off. If there is not a proper scheme of maintenance it can result in guest dissatisfaction. Some establishments choose a system of preventative maintenance—the replacement of one light bulb can be more expensive than replacing all in a room or area at once at a planned time before the expected failure.

Because of the public nature of a hotel many things can happen that influence maintenance. When this occurs it creates costs that may not be scheduled. The objective is to convert unplanned maintenance into planned maintenance. But this is not always possible. This is particularly true in situations of a dangerous nature, or situations where dealing with a maintenance issue quickly will reduce long-term costs, or where the lack of a quick response will impact guest satisfaction. For example, although electric lights have an average life expectancy, this does not guarantee that they will not fail much earlier. This could impact the safety of employees and guests. As a result, unplanned maintenance is not merely desirable; it is a factor that must be taken into account as part of operations planning.

HOUSEKEEPING

The management of facilities is not simply deciding what facilities will be made available to the guest. The way the facilities of the hotel are maintained is of vital importance. Research by Lockyer (2003) discusses facilities and cleanliness, and in particular draws the reader's attention to the impact that such factors as smell, toilets, windows, and even curtains have on guests. The constant day-to-day effort to ensure that the facilities of the hotel are maintained in a condition appropriate for the establishment is an essential part of the work of housekeeping. "These essential services are often not given the importance they deserve in management texts, and are considered to be somewhat unglamorous" (Powers, 1995, p. 255). The housekeeping department is the only one that keeps regular liaisons with every other department and department head in the property. "They are the 'eyes and ears' of management; they will see and hear things that often the manager will miss" (Schneider & Tucker, 1989, p. 37). This makes their interactions with other departments very important. For example, the housekeeping department communicates with reception for such information as the occupancy, status of rooms, requirements of guests. They communicate with the restaurant in relation to the linen requirements and its exchange. They communicate with maintenance to report and get information. They communicate with purchasing to ensure supplies and cleaning materials are available. They communicate with accounting in relation to hours worked and salaries. They communicate with security in relation to keys, lost property and overall security of the premises. In addition, the housekeeping department is responsible for the overall cleanliness and maintenance of standards throughout the hotel.

The housekeeping department is often seen as the one that takes care of cleaning the bedrooms, making the beds, emptying the garbage cans, and putting out clean towels; but it is a lot more extensive than that. This department is often responsible for everything from the selection of fabrics to the selection and purchase of all the furniture. If housekeeping needs to maintain standards in the property, they need to ensure that the items purchased can be cleaned and preserved in their best possible condition. There are many stories in the hotel industry about the "disasters" that have occurred when a new hotel has been designed by professional architects who have specified furniture and other fittings that look wonderful but are very difficult to clean and maintain. Some years ago a well-known international hotel in Hong Kong was refurbished. All the bedroom furniture had a thin decorative copper strip inserted into the wood. This looked wonderful at first but consideration was not given to how it could be kept clean. Using normal brass cleaner damaged the wood and discolored it. Using normal wood polish did not clean the brass. Housekeeping spent many hours trying to clean the brass without damaging the wood, using a small toothbrush.

The hotel's housekeeper is, as a result of the broad responsibilities, a very important person amongst the staff.

How valuable is the housekeeper to maintaining the standards in the hotel?

I employ a very good housekeeper who terrifies me. I think housekeepers were meant to scare management. They have always had a myth about them. When I came here we had two head housekeepers, both Scottish and they were very fastidious in their demands and standards. I think you can get away with a lot of things in a hotel but one of the things you can't get away with is a lack of cleanliness. Consequently you employ the people who can do that job—one of the hard jobs to fill these days is chambermaids—not everyone wants to clean someone's toilet or change soiled sheets.

(Terry Holmes, Executive Director,
The Stafford, London)

Despite the importance of housekeeping to the satisfaction of the guests and repeat business, the housekeeping staff are often low paid, temporary employees. An industry measure is that in a quality property approximately ten to fifteen guest bedrooms can be cleaned per shift (Branson & Lennox, 1989). Productivity is greatly impacted by the fluctuation in occupancy and discussed in the chapter on yield management. In a property with 1,000 rooms, the occupancy could easily change by 4 or 5 percent from one night to the next, which represents a variance of forty or fifty rooms and a related fluctuation in housekeeping staff needs.

In addition to maintaining the cleanliness and maintenance of the hotel property, the housekeeping department has responsibilities to operate within legal requirements. Although these change significantly from country to country, they can include

- fire precaution regulations;
- health and safety at work regulations;
- food hygiene regulations;
- employment legislation; and
- accident reporting and prevention.

Not only do these requirements have an impact on guest satisfaction, not fulfilling these requirements according to regulations can result in legal action being taken by external bodies.

OUTSOURCING

In the competitive and difficult environment in which hotels operate outsourcing can assist with operations from food and beverage provision to guests, security, cleaning and maintenance, down to lesser significant aspects such as vending machine provision (Hemmington & King, 2000). The reasons for outsourcing are varied and include seasonal fluctuations, staff skill shortages, manpower shortages, space and facility shortages, lack of specialty knowledge, changes in trends and fashions, and cost consideration.

Outsourcing—is this new?

In the Shenzhen market it is just developing. In other countries you have a very mature market but in China it just started. Manpower is expensive but we need high occupancy to cover the costs. We take the outsourcing company's staff, we train them, but we pay them per day per hour. We pay higher than we would pay our own people but we have no need to pay dormitory, insurance, and so on. This gives us greater flexibility.

(Ralph Wong, Rooms Division,
Crowne Plaza, Shenzhen, China)

An example of ways that outsourcing is used in the housekeeping department include:

- Linen and laundry services—because of the need for a large investment in equipment and space
- Periodic cleaning—due to specific additional work required such as carpet shampooing or sanding of wood floors that requires specialized equipment
- Pest control—because of use of specialized chemicals and specific knowledge
- Window cleaning—difficulty with accessibility creating hazardous tasks, which require specialized knowledge and equipment

However, while the reduction of cost is often cited as the most pressing need for the use of outsourcing, the true impact on the financial cost and a robust evaluation of the comparison of costs is often not undertaken.

Is your outsourcing a cost savings to you?

It is easier and has a cost savings also. I don't have to have employees, or give them a bonus, or whatever. The scale of operations works better for me.

(P. S. Ramdas, Managing Director,
Tourist Home [Pvt.] Ltd, Egmore, Chennai, India)

Before considering outsourcing a full investigation of what is currently being done needs to be undertaken. The purpose of this investigation is to measure the level of current satisfaction and to determine if a change would be beneficial. Such a review may include the following questions:

- Is the current provision of the product or service efficient and cost effective?
- How could the provision of goods and services from an outsource supplier be compared with the current offering?

- Are the customers currently satisfied, and would a change ensure ongoing satisfaction?
- How do competitive establishments handle outsourcing?
- Is the provision of quality from an outsource supply guaranteed in the medium and long term?

The impact of any change must be looked at very carefully; management needs assurance that any change in the way in which goods or services are provided will not harm the quality of the overall product and that it will be financially beneficial. There needs to be an ongoing evaluation of the positives and negatives of outsourcing. Part of this involves the evaluation of the hotel's core business and expertise. It is therefore necessary to identify the core competencies on which the organization's ongoing success and survival is based, and then to determine what impact outsourcing may have on the core business.

There are a number of situations in which outsourcing may not be the most appropriate action.

- When the cost of outsourcing is higher than providing in-house
- When it is strategically important to maintain in-house provision
- When changing to outsourcing may have a major impact on existing employees
- When the ability to monitor and measure outsourcing performance is difficult

There are two parts to an outsourcing agreement: the service specification and the service level. The service specification must be complete and unambiguous. It is important that all parties clearly understand and can put into writing exactly what service is required. If this is not done it becomes impossible to measure the level of service provided and variance from the required standard. On the other hand, there is a danger of being overly specific and as a result, making the agreement too complex and doomed to failure. Therefore, a balance needs to be obtained.

SUMMARY

This chapter brings together a number of important management issues. As in other chapters, the intention is not to be exhaustive in the discussion, but rather to raise the issue and allow the reader to develop his or her own thoughts, ideas, and analysis. The underlying importance is the value of the setting and measurement of standards. These standards and the variation of them flow throughout the operations in a hotel. Management must understand the standards and the environment in which it is operating so that it can maximize effectiveness and return. These include issues such as the age of the property, its condition, purchasing of goods, and so on.

This chapter also discussed the importance of maintaining the assets within the hotel. Purchasing systems need to be developed so they can be appropriately managed. This is particularly true because of the changing needs and wants of the hotel guest. Health and safety is a constant issue that can make a hotel legally liable if not adhered to. This is not only for customers, but also for employees. Appropriate training and guidance must be given. The manager of the hotel is often required to work with the owners of the hotel, which can require a great deal of time and effort as owners may play a very active role in the management of the establishment. Good relationships with management can make purchases of facilities and equipment and expenditure a lot easier. The question of hotel life cycles, as well as being directly related to yield management, needs to be understood. Housekeeping has an important role in the day-to-day maintenance of the standards of the hotel, as well as an important communication relationship with many parts of the hotel. It plays a very important (and sometimes not sufficiently recognized) part in the profitability of the establishment.

DISCUSSION

A. Identify and discuss five or six standards that could be established; include how variance from such standards could be measured.
B. Evaluate in what areas of a hotel variance analysis can be applied and the way in which that analysis may be used.
C. From the perspective of a hotel's general manager, evaluate techniques that can be used to control the cost of purchasing.
D. Visit a hotel in your vicinity and evaluate what actions the housekeeping department takes in relation to maintaining guest health and safety issues.

E. What major issues do you see in relation to the management of hotel property owners; what ways could you better manage these issues?

F. Identify a selection of hotels in your area, and categorize at what stage they are in as it relates to the hotel life cycle, and the impact this has on refurbishment.

G. What advantages and/or disadvantages do you see to maintenance planning?

H. The housekeeping department is key to the quality of a hotel; evaluate this statement.

I. Identify to what extent hotels use outsourcing in your region, discussing advantages and disadvantages.

CASE STUDIES

Case Study 5.1. The Cresswell Hotel

Aggie Mackie has recently been appointed executive head housekeeper at the Cresswell Hotel, in Dumfries, Scotland. She thought when she was appointed that that the hotel was very neat and clean and so was looking forward to her new post.

On the second day of her employment she got in just as the cleaning staff were arriving and soon realized there were major problems with the department.

On walking along the corridors at 8:00 am she encountered two of her staff (who she later discovered were called Dawn and Jen) pulling their trolley along the corridor, shouting "housekeeping, housekeeping" very loudly as they went. Dawn was dressed in the hotel regulation overall, but was wearing a cardigan over the top and a pair of slippers. Jen's hair was loose and hung down past her shoulders. She watched Dawn approach a "Do Not Disturb" sign on a bedroom door, read it, and then knock on the door and enter the room using her master key. She also watched her retreat back to the corridor quickly when a woman's scream rent the air. The pair carried on in much the same way, trying to find a room they could get into.

Intrigued, Aggie continued to follow their actions, as she was new, they clearly did not know who she was. They eventually found an occupied room that the guests had recently left to spend some time sightseeing. They parked their trolley outside the door and started their cleaning routine. First of all they switched on the television, pulled the bedcovers up so that the bed looked made and Jen went into the bathroom to start work there. Using the guest hand towel, first of all she wiped the toilet bowl and then, with the same cloth, the bath, the wash hand basin, the shelf, the glasses, and finally the coffee cups. She then folded the towel, so the coffee marks did not show and replaced it on the heated towel rail. Before leaving the room she had a squirt from the perfume bottle that clearly belonged to the guest, gave her teeth a quick brush with the guests' toothbrush, and applied some lipstick, also belonging to the guest.

Meanwhile Dawn was concentrating her efforts in the bedroom. She pulled the vacuum cleaner in and proceeded to vacuum the floor. It did not appear to be working very well as the whole vacuuming process made very little difference to the carpet. She then found a rather grubby duster on the trolley and flicked it around the furniture, before sitting down on the bed to watch an interesting part of morning television. After about ten minutes of TV, they were finished in the room and left slamming the door behind them, leaving the duster on the bedside table.

Aggie went to find the assistant housekeeper (Kim) responsible for the area and after a bit of searching, she found her on another floor cleaning the bedrooms there. Aggie was aware that they were a little short staffed but not to the extent where the supervisory staff had to do the cleaner's work so her first question was to enquire why Kim was cleaning. Kim replied rather vaguely that there was too much work to cover, so she liked to lend a hand. Aggie then quizzed her about Dawn and Jen's behavior. Her reply was that they were rather troublesome and she had attempted to train them but all they did was giggle and say they had their own way of working and no one ever complained about their work. She also added that they were great fun in the canteen and on nights out they were the "life and soul of the party."

Aggie then continued her way around the hotel and found that although one or two of the other cleaners had a similar working technique to Dawn and Jen, others worked quite differently and in a more organized manner. They followed a routine where they paired up to make beds, but after that worked on their own, cleaning bedrooms and corridors in an effective way, following all the rules of good hygiene, and the (economical) use of cleaning agents, equipment, and materials. They dressed neatly in their overalls and wore sensible shoes and had their hair styled neatly and tied back where necessary.

Judith E. Brown BA, MA, ILTM, FRSA,
School of Sport and Leisure,
Gloucester University, Cheltenham, England

Questions

1. The problems that occur in the Cresswell Hotel are quite obvious from the case study, but what are the reasons for the occurrence of these problems?
2. What would you recommend to Aggie to sort out the problems?
3. What other issues are evident for the overall operation of the hotel?

Case Study 5.2. Impact of Seasons

The following is from an interview with the General Manager of the Grand America Hotel in Salt Lake City, Utah. Salt Lake City is situated in the rocky mountains (4330 ft. above sea level) and is subject to very cold winter temperatures (a low of 19 °F in January and a high of 93 °F in July).

In this hotel we have a wide variety of temperatures. We are prepared for four main seasons; we need snow blowers for the wintertime and deicers to take care of the building. We have a very sophisticated energy system. We are a newer building, finished right before the Olympics in 2002. The owner built it for the Olympics and he wanted it to have a real European feel—most of the fixtures are from Europe, all the artwork from throughout Europe, carpets from England, chandeliers from Milan. There is an immense cost of building something like this.

Bruce Fery, General Manager,
Grand America Hotel, Salt Lake City

Questions

1. Evaluate what impact a rapidly changing four seasons has on a hotel's housekeeping department.
2. Identify a hotel locally; consider what impacts the climate has on the hotel's maintenance.
3. What specific differences do you believe age would have on the maintenance in a hotel?

Case Study 5.3. Maintenance of Standards

Crowne Plaza Shenzhen is the first 5-star business-leisure theme hotel in China. The theme is based on Venice. It is a global business hotel. Advertising material states the hotel is located in the southwest of Shenzhen city, right next to the famous Window of the World, Splendid China, China Folk Culture Villages theme parks, and Happy Kingdom, the hotel is one or two minutes away from Futian Center and the Hi-Tech Zone, twenty minutes away from Shekou Harbor Passenger Terminal and twenty-five minutes away from Lo Wu Port and Shenzhen International Airport. The following information is from an interview with the general manager:

At the moment we are the number one hotel in China out of forty hotels. As far as guest feedback is concerned we are number one, our housekeeping is rated number one by the guests and we set a very high standard. We are preparing for some new competitors coming into the market, within the next year-and-a-half so we are trying to improve further on where we are. Our housekeeper—she has done a great job in regard to our cleanliness, we are regarded as number one in cleanliness—she requested a transfer to another hotel which we will arrange for her and we are going to replace her with an expatriate, not because we feel we have a problem—we don't—but because we feel we are number one but let's move to another level. The new properties opening try to attract our staff but the salary range is lower than ours, so they try to get our supervisors and make them assistant managers, our assistant managers to become managers. That is how we lose some staff, but fortunately not too many.

Peter Pollmeier, General Manager,
Crowne Plaza, Shenzhen, China

Questions

1. Evaluate the relationship between the employees of the hotel and the management of resources.
2. Investigate a hotel locally and consider the impact that the house-keeping department has on the overall hotel.
3. Discuss how variance analysis could be used in this case.

REFERENCES

Branson, J.C., & Lennox, M. (1989). *Hotel, hostel, and hospital housekeeping* (5th ed.). London: Hodder & Stoughton.

Feldman, D.S. (1995). Asset management: Here to stay. *Cornell Hotel and Restaurant Administration Quarterly, 36*(5), 36-52.

Hemmington, N., & King, C. (2000). Key dimensions of outsourcing hotel food and beverage services. *International Journal of Contemporary Hospitality Management, 12*(4), 256.

Jagels, M.G., & Coltman, M.M. (2004). *Hospitality management accounting,* (8th ed.). Hoboken, New Jersey: John Wiley & Sons.

Jones, C. (2002). Facilities management in medium-sized UK hotels. *International Journal of Contemporary Hospitality Management, 14*(2), 72-80.

Jones, C., & Jowett, V. (1998). *Managing facilities.* Oxford: Butterworth Heinemann.

Kreck, L.A. (1978). *Operational problem solving for the hotel and restaurant industry.* Boston, MA: CBI Publishing Company, Inc.

Lawson, F. (1995). *Hotels & Resorts.* London: Architectural Press.

Lockyer, T. (2003). Hotel cleanliness: How do guests view it? Let's get specific. *The International Journal of Hospitality Management, 22*(3), 297-305.

Loether, J. (2005). Meeting technology in on the move; plan for future. *Hotel and Motel Management, 220*(4), 14.

Powers, T. (1995). *Introduction to management in the hospitality industry.* New York: John Wiley & Sons, Inc.

Rushmore, S. (1992). Hotel life expectancy. *Lodging Hospitality, 48*(5), 16.

Schneider, M., & Tucker, G. (1989). *The professional housekeeper.* New York: Van Nostrand Reinhold.

Chapter 6

Yield Management

> The worst thing that the hotel industry did was to teach their guests to expect discounts.

CHAPTER OBJECTIVES

On completion of this chapter the reader will understand:

- the environment required for the use of yield management
- the definition of yield management
- the way in which yield management is used in today's management environment
- the impact that aggressive use of yield management can have in the long term on sustainability
- the way in which the Internet has influenced yield management, and how management can control the negatives of the electronic environment
- the relationship between yield management and guest satisfaction

Key Word Definitions

economy of scale: Reduction in cost per unit resulting from increased production, realized through operational efficiencies.

occupancy percent: The percentage of rooms occupied on a daily, weekly, or yearly basis, mathematically defined as rooms sold divided by the rooms available.

The International Hotel Industry: Sustainable Management
© 2007 by The Haworth Press, Inc. All rights reserved.
doi:10.1300/5869_07

price inelastic: The low influence that a price change has on the buyer's decision to purchase a product or service.

rack rates: A term that comes from the use of the Whitney System, commonly used before computerized systems were introduced into hotels. In this system there were racks where the various pieces of information relating to rooms and price were stored.

SARS: Severe Acute Respiratory Syndrome.

yield management: Mathematically defined as actual revenue divided by potential revenue multiplied by 100, also commonly defined as selling the right room, to the right person for the right price.

Chapter Review

For a hotel manager the understanding, implementation, and use of yield management is an important issue as it can greatly influence both the short- and long-term success and even survival of a hotel (Okumus, 2004). Although yield management has been used for many years in the aviation industry, its use in the hotel industry is still reasonably new and in many respects is not well understood. The purpose of this chapter is to define and give examples of the use of yield management along with emphasizing current issues that influence the decision making surrounding yield management. The discussion emphasizes the impact that a pricing strategy has on the sustainability of a business, along with such issues as the impact that yield management has on hotel guest perception and satisfaction and how the Internet has influenced the way managers deal with the pricing issue. In addition, emphasis is placed on the overuse of price variation to control occupancy and the pitfalls of such action. The chapter also emphasizes the need of a yield management culture to be developed in a hotel for it to succeed (Higley, 2003). The discussion covers the positive aspects of the use of yield management, and also gives emphasis to the negatives.

It must be noted that in parts of the world "revenue management" is used in place of "yield management" and has the same meaning. For the purpose of this book "yield management" will be used exclusively. Many hotels have revenue managers, either individuals or whole departments whose job is to analyze and make recommendations on pricing strategies.

INTRODUCTION TO THEORY:
YIELD MANAGEMENT

Yield management in a hotel is a technique for managers to focus on obtaining the maximum return or yield for the investment in the space in the hotel (Berman, 2005). It can be defined as selling the right inventory (the room or space in the hotel) to the right customer for the right price at the right time (Smith, Leimkuhler, & Darrow, 1992), and yield management is about doing exactly that. However, it is a much more complex issue for managers than this definition may suggest. The objective is to focus management decision making not on simply selling rooms but selling rooms in such a way that would make the most financial return for the hotel.

To successfully use the principles of yield management, hotel managers must achieve an understanding of the market in which they are operating. They also have to achieve a long-term vision of the hotel's future so as to not be enticed into deciding on a short-term gain that could detrimentally affect the long-term sustainability of the property. This reflects a change in management direction toward a need for managers to be aware of and promote sustainability. This means the hotel does not merely exist from one year to the next but that the environment and actions of management make the hotel a sound entity for all parties, from the staff employed to the investors in the property. The principles of yield management are not solely applicable to room sales as the same principles can be applied in other areas of the hotel (Okumus, 2004).

Yield management and computer systems are often linked together in discussions and in the literature, giving the feeling that these two things are inseparably related, suggesting perhaps that yield management decisions become a mechanical part of the hotel's computer system (Overby, 2005). In such a diverse industry, this approach is an oversimplification, as for yield management to be successful, it is as much art as science, with a large diversity of approaches (Koide & Ishii, 2005; Okumus, 2004). It is therefore important to ensure the involvement of staff so that yield management does not become just the application of a mathematical formula (Lieberman, 1993).

There are two commonly used measures that specifically look at the hotel room and its uses:

1. Average room occupancy—number of rooms available divided by the number of occupied rooms.
2. Average room rate—total revenue from rooms divided by the number of rooms occupied.

The problem faced by hotel managers is that while each of these figures is important, each has an influence on the other. The question that must be answered by hotel management is whether to sell a large number of rooms for one night at low rates (this has the effect of reducing the average room rate), or holding out for room sales at published (or higher) rack rates (this would result in high room rate but low occupancy).

Yield management—how do you deal with that?

We have a revenue manager, similar to any other hotel. You have to look at the business in different segmentations, and the buying behaviors within that segmentation. Then all that has to be measured up against the positioning of the hotel. Just a couple of months ago we were having a conversation with our reservations team, asking if we could do more business in terms of bodies and room nights if the room rate was $50, and the answer unequivocally is "yes," there are more people who would fit into that filtration mechanism and come to stay. Not that there is anything wrong with people who only want to pay $50 but that's a different position for this resort. Instead if a resort decides to charge $250 where there is more filtration that has to come through, price in itself filters some of the people out because everyone has a different disposable income. So you look at the demand that is going to be there and any typical patterns that might be there. On top of that if you have any specific events that are going on that are going to target the more affluent than possibly the more rate sensitive folks, and then the decision has to be made on what to sell and how to position for that time period, the driver being the demand.

(Abid Butt, General Manager,
Turtle Bay Resort, Hawaii)

In contrast to the previous approach, yield management works by using the formula revenue realized divided by revenue potential.

The revenue realized is a variable and the revenue potential is generally fixed (as long as the same number of rooms is available).

Yield management was first used by the airline industry following airline deregulation in the United States in the 1970s. The objective as defined by American Airlines (Smith, Leimkubler, & Darrow, 1992, p. 22) was "to maximize passenger revenue by selling the right seats to the right customers at the right time." The requirements of yield management are (1) high fixed costs, and (2) low variable costs. In relation to an airline, there is the high cost of the purchase of the aircraft, and a low variable cost per seat. The same characteristics are present in the hotel industry where there is a high cost of building the facility and a low cost of servicing the room. The marginal cost of selling one additional room is (or at least can be) low, as these costs are related items such as the cleaning of the room and the laundry, which are generally low costs. Traditional management theory and logic suggests that as long as the revenue covers all variable costs and contributes to fixed costs in the short term, the room could be sold at a discounted rate. However, this approach has a number of problems associated with it (Higley, 2003), as will be seen later.

Yield management has two parts:

1. A differential room rate pricing strategy—the price charged to a guest in any particular situation.
2. Room inventory management—allocating different types of rooms to the pattern of demand.

Finding the balance between these two has impacts upon the sustainability of the hotel property and on guest level of satisfaction, and is a far more complex question than may be initially anticipated. It requires considerable research and an in-depth understanding of the market in which the hotel is operating.

How do you approach yield management?

We have a revenue director and personal assistant and then we have a total revenue management team, and we get together every Tuesday. The members of the team are myself, director of marketing, the revenue director, director of catering, director of computer services, director of room services and some other people to talk about whatever the topic is going to be. We discuss our group business, we look at what the competition is doing, we look at what kind of response we are getting for our products, we look at results for the different channels for the hotel. We measure all that.

(Octavio Gamarra, General Manager,
Ritz-Carlton Millenia, Singapore)

The Ritz-Carlton is a large (600+ rooms) luxury hotel and needs to undertake extensive research. The process is no less important to the following fifty-four room hotel in India, but it is interesting to see how this manager handles the aspect of assessing his competition.

What research do you undertake in relation to your competitors?

In the evening when I drive past, I always look into other hotels. If you have lights on in a lot of rooms then you can estimate their occupancy. I can look at the hotel and tell how well they are doing. My work boys (outsourcing staff) come here, and I ask them. If I see someone from another hotel close to mine, I will ask him how are things going. Sometimes they do not tell you right—I go by in the evening and I know things are not as they say.

(P. S. Ramdas, Managing Director,
Tourist Home [Pvt.] Ltd, Egmore, Chennai, India)

In addition to techniques such as observing what the competitors are doing to promote occupancy, there are a number of software packages that electronically enquire of computer reservation databases and retrieve the competitors pricing strategies and then produce reports comparing the prices.

How much time is spent finding out what your competitors are doing?

Very little time because there are only four or five hotels that are closely competitive with us, in the secondary environment there are ten to thirteen hotels that are competitive in different segmentations of the market. With ecommerce and the GDS [Global Distribution System] and Internet in this environment now, getting information is not difficult because with the rate view program, that shows two rates and four channels and you create a report. And besides that you always have the three-month report, and the up to thirty days occupancy report. We can easily deduce what to sell from our own data on the market.

(William Chu, Director, Revenue Strategy,
Ritz-Carlton Millenia, Singapore)

ROOM RATE AND OCCUPANCY

Changing room rates is a strategy that management often uses to try to maximize revenue. Depending on the objective of management the room rate can either be increased or decreased. The success of increasing the room rate depends on the elasticity of the market and the availability of an increase in the number of customers (Brewton, 1991). The hotel industry in most situations can be classified as "purely competitive"—the characteristics of such a market are that there are a large number of producers, similarity among products, entry and exit from the industry is easy, purchasers have a perfect knowledge of the market, and purchasers and sellers have no collusion (Melotte, 1995).

Operators fearful of loosing market share use price cutting to the point that it becomes a ruinous tactic in an effort to induce travel and increase occupancy (Arnold, 1994). This has resulted in a reversal of the concept of economy of scale. Economy of scale is defined as reduction in cost per unit resulting from increased production, realized through operational efficiencies. In the reverse, the effect is an increase in cost per unit, with an increased level of sales. While the number of rooms occupied has increased, which has increased the variable total cost, the amount of profit per room has decreased. As a result, rate cuts have generated more revenue but not necessarily additional profit (Arnold, 1994). To overcome the reduction in the profit from rooms some hotels have increased prices in other parts of the hotel with the objective of reversing the declining room profit. For example, charging $38 for a modest breakfast in a New York hotel (Marshall, 1995). Because of the hotel's desire to increase occupancy, and the use of discounts to aid in this, the hotel industry has educated the traveling public to shop for discounts and bargains (Feiertag, 1992).

Pricing is different depending upon the market the hotel is operating in. Nevertheless, the correct pricing strategy should be followed for a particular type of hotel property.

What is your philosophy in relation to yield management? What are the things you are doing in this very competitive market to make it successful?

Ritz-Carlton is in the luxury frame and the pricing must always be correct. There are three steps of pricing that I have developed in order to be competitive in the market. You do need to know the price of the competitors, but first of all, the first step is rational pricing, followed by sectional pricing. So as long as you get rational pricing correct you fit into the competitive environment, at the right rate for the right product, you will be able to sell better with higher market penetration than the competitors. Sectional pricing—you need to sell where there is demand for certain packages or promotions, not so much as a seasonal feel but more segmentation. The third one covers seasonality, where you move your prices up and down according to demand and supply.

(William Chu, Director Revenue Strategy,
Ritz-Carlton Millenia, Singapore)

The pricing in many hotels can involve as many as ten or fifteen room rates for each hotel (Koss, 1992; Gijsbrechts, 1993). Two of the issues to be considered in relation to changes in room prices are the number of increases in room rate in any one year, and the number of places where room rates are listed. Fluctuating prices too rapidly may lead to customer rejection (Brewton, 1991).

To assist in the understanding of the factors influencing hotel room price, reference can be made to classical microeconomic theory that looks at the different factors that impact the price of accommodations. A model of hotel room pricing was suggested by Ellerbrock Hite and Wells (1984), in which they suggested nine factors that influence the price charged by a hotel. These included

1. the average room rate charged by other hotels in the region,
2. the fixed costs of the hotel,
3. the variable costs of the hotel,
4. the cost of advertising,
5. the value of the location,
6. the amenities available in the hotel,
7. the occupancy percentage of hotels in the competing region,
8. the amount of competition from other hotels, and
9. the season of the year, time, or special events impacting on price.

In the model by Ellerbrock, Hite, and Wells (1984), particular focus is placed on the variable cost. "Profit is maximized by setting price such that the marginal revenue received from renting the last room equals the marginal cost of renting the room" (Ellerbrock, Hite, & Wells, 1984, p. 12). The marginal costs of any room influences the number of rooms that an operator is willing to make available for rental up to a maximum of those available.

Hotel prices are often set without an understanding of consumer perceptions of price (Zeithaml & Bitner, 1996). The pricing for service industries faces three complicating factors: Hotel guests find it difficult to reference the price of services; guests believe hotel quality is indicated by price; the hotel service product contains many parts which are not always reflected in the price. These relate to the intangibility of the product as discussed earlier. The first factor depends on frequency of use—arguably business users have experience with prices but it could be the demand is price inelastic, or less sensitive to changes, if a corporation is paying.

Another approach is the use of incentives to build occupancy—while there is considerable risk in cutting prices in the face of tough competition, risk can be minimized by using price incentives. These build occupancy without eroding profits because they are aimed at attracting new customers or additional sales from existing customers (Brewton, 1991).

A pricing method often suggested is that of $1 charged for every $1,000 of development price (Lewis & Shoemaker, 1997). Using this model, a room that cost $100,000 to develop would have a daily rate of $100. This is often used as a basic concept and although is considered a "rule of thumb" (Mullen, 1998), has little application. This approach is referred to as "cost-driven pricing." Although giving some indication of the price for a room, cost-driven pricing has also been criticized as an approach to setting prices (Shaw, 1992). The establishment of a rack price involves a number of issues—most of these involve a price-driven costing approach.

In setting the rack price a reference pricing process may be involved. This is the price of any service that a consumer thinks of as an appropriate price for that item (Lewis & Shoemaker, 1997). This price can comprise "the price last paid, the price most frequently paid, or the average of all prices customers have paid for similar offerings" (Zeithaml & Bitner, 1996, p. 486).

How do you deal with pricing?

Singapore is a very competitive market so you look at yourself within the context of your competitive set. We look at our key competitors as far as benchmarking ourselves and we consistently beat them by anywhere from $20-38. We do it because we don't sell on price, we sell on the value that you receive when you stay here. When business travelers come and stay here there is a certain commodity that they have very little of, and that is time. They come and stay here because our service has a direct impact on the productiveness they can achieve during their stay, say the two-and-a-half days that they are here. From the time between their wake up call and their breakfast arrives ... there are a thousand little things that must be right and are taken for granted, but when they are wrong will render them less productive (the air conditioning not working, their cereal and fruit not being right, not having a comfortable bed, and not receiving a wake up call that is friendly, personal, and timely). This hotel is quietly efficient. I refer to our department heads and staff as a precision-drill team, and so we are part of our guests' lives and success. They may spend another $50-60 Singapore for the twenty-four hours they are with us, which in the context of an international trip is nothing (most of them are flying business or first class). We run a pretty good occupancy and a higher average rate.

(Christopher Norton, Regional Vice President/GM,
Four Seasons Hotel, Singapore)

Pricing for services is more difficult for consumers to identify than pricing for products. Consumers often know how much they paid for a television or a bag of sugar, but a hotel room is quite a different issue in their minds (Lewis & Shoemaker, 1997). A major reason is the variability across services (size of room, facilities offered, level of service, and other features), whereas a bag of sugar is tangible and can be clearly seen and judged by the consumer. This lack of a clear reference makes it complex for consumers to establish a firm reference point for pricing service purchases.

A study undertaken by Morley (1994) examines the multidimensional nature of the tourism price. Morley (1994, p. 8) reports that "Practitioners in tourism marketing have stated to the author that potential tourists facing such a complexity of prices focus their attention on the larger cost items, particularly airfares for long distance touring." The article reports on an investigation of the effects of some tourism price components on potential tourist choice of destination using a multinomial logit model analysis of stated choice frequencies. Three factors investigated in relation to tourists originating from Kuala Lumpur and traveling to Australia indicate airfare has the most significant effect on the choice of tourism. Hotel rate and exchange rates of ± 15 percent have a smaller impact (Morley, 1994).

PRICING STRATEGIES

An aspect of hotel pricing strategies is the impact that a short-term gain may have on the long-term survival of the property. It may be argued that the combination of low occupancy and high room rates, or high occupancy and low room rates are equally desirable, ignoring for the moment the potential sales revenue that may be generated in other outlets in the hotel by following a policy of high occupancy and low room rate. They clearly are not equal, as a policy of high occupancy and low room rate may in the short term give some satisfactory returns, however in the long term it also can be disastrous. Each time a hotel room is occupied, there is deterioration of that facility. This may be very small and not visible on a day-to-day basis but is evident in the long term.

Do you find that the problem with high occupancy is that the rooms deteriorate and if you are not charging enough to maintain the facilities and quality of rooms, over time the quality of the hotel tends to decline and so you have to charge less?

A lot of the hotels, particularly in Malaysia, are experiencing cash flow problems and when you have a cash flow problem, you would rather sell a little bit lower so you would have enough cash turn around. But again the owners have their ideas. A lot of hotel managers now are being so-called detected by the owners. The owners have a direct involvement in hotels, becoming more obvious now for the past five years. A hotel general manager may want to achieve the highest rate because he needs money to improve the product. We tried this once, raised rates, then got "shot down" by the owner when the occupancy dropped. The owner was looking directly at occupancy percentages only.

(Nash Nasihin Ali, General Manager,
Mutiara Hotel, Johor, Malaysia)

MARKET SEGMENTATION

Part of yield management is selling to the right person. Although this is discussed in the chapter on marketing, the segmentation of the market has a direct impact on the amount charged for a particular room, with any particular market being segmented in a variety of different ways (Ladany, 2001).

One way in which this is being done is through the use of electronic pricing on the Internet (DaCosta, 2001), but this may not be the best approach. For a fuller discussion refer to the chapter on marketing.

EXTERNAL INFLUENCES

There are a number of models available for the determination of decisions that maximize yield in a hotel, and these vary from simply being based on time and vacancies to extensively more complex models (Badinelli, 2000). A major part of yield management is the monitoring of the environment in which the hotel is operating. This involves being aware of and monitoring the influence that events have on the hotel; these vary widely in their nature from local and national holidays, special tourist events, issues affecting other local properties, introduction of new rooms into the market, and weather, right through things like industrial action in areas such as airlines and railways and even hospitals. The application of yield management is also influenced by management and other staff in the hotel and their view of yield management's implementation and its effectiveness (Okumus, 2004). This also includes major disruptions such as SARS, terrorism, natural disasters, bird flu, and so on.

What happened with SARS?

Our occupancy didn't go that low. At that time we were still doing 40 percent average occupancy. Some Singapore hotels were hit very badly, some doing single digits. SARS or not, we still have business travelers. Where hotels were dependent so much on the leisure market, they were hit hard by SARS. We were fortunate. Normally we would have done 60-65 percent, so it did drop off but not too much. At the very lowest it was 38 percent.

(Nash Nasihin Ali, General Manager,
Mutiara Hotel, Johor, Malaysia)

Have things changed since 9/11?

Incentive travel has changed. After 9/11 all of the corporate travel dried up overnight, so a lot of the incentives were not in place. For about a year or so that incentive market virtually went away. As the recovery started the incentives were put back into place to gain the revenues by the companies, but certainly not as lavishly as they were done before 9/11, definitely smaller. Here in North American terms there is another example—there have been a lot of legislative changes after the debacle of ENRON and WORLCOM—a lot of the major Fortune 500 companies are under major scrutiny. In the past, when there was an incentive where the CEO would put you up and charter a plane, well, those days are gone.

(Abid Butt, General Manager,
Turtle Bay Resort, Hawaii)

Because of all these events, many of them external to the hotel, constant monitoring is important. Many hotels will regularly phone other properties pretending they are potential guests and enquire about the amount being charged for a room. Other hotels use software that electronically searches Internet Web sites, and collates the prices being charged. One technique used in yield management is discounts for early booking. Although this adds some security of occupancy, it requires careful monitoring of overbooking policies (preset percentages) and it reduces the ability of the hotel to make decisions close to the time that external events may influence occupancy (Koide & Ishii, 2005).

A useful way to view yield management and the multiple influences that impact the decision process is from a systems perspective. In short, a systems approach to decision making looks at the influence that the different parts of an organization, in this case a hotel, has on yield management decisions. The effectiveness of yield management may be impacted by these factors. As already indicated these influences can be external to the hotel or within the hotel. For example, unwillingness in certain quarters for staff to make decisions.

How do staff handle decision making within the hotel?

In China it is not an easy matter. We like to say we empower staff, but if you look at rank and file staff, it is quite difficult to say you are allowed to make decisions worth a given amount. Staff still feel that they need to check with the supervisor, supervisor with manager, and so on. I don't think it is really happening here. A supervisor is able to write off a meal ticket, give a bottle of wine—those things are assigned regularly. But the rank and file staff are difficult to get to that level because they are not used to making decisions. Division Heads are fully empowered. They make decisions; as long as they keep me informed about what is going on I don't want them to check with me on day-to-day operations.

(David Lim, Executive Assistant Manager,
Crowne Plaza, Shenzhen, China)

This impacts the effectiveness of yield management. For a fuller discussion of the use of yield management and systems analysis see Jones (1999).

OTHER HOTEL OPERATIONS

In relation to the requirements for yield management, high fixed costs and low variable costs lend themselves very well to the sale of rooms in a hotel as previously discussed. However, what about other operations in a hotel, do they have similar characteristics so that they can benefit from the use of yield management?

In regard to yield management in relation to the room only, Kimes (1999, p. 17) expands this to restaurants as "selling the right seat to the right customer at the right price and for the right duration." The determination of "right" entails achieving both the most revenue possible for the restaurant and also delivering the greatest value or utility to the customer. Without that balance, yield management practices will in the long term alienate those customers who will feel that the restaurant has taken advantage of them.

A restaurant in general, and specifically a restaurant in a hotel, has a lot of its cost tied up in the space occupied and the equipment. The space allocated to a restaurant influences the return on the investment in the hotel. If it does not give an appropriate return it may be better converting it for another use such as a conference room. The better utilization of the facility raises many of the same questions as in room utilization. In short, how can the asset of the restaurant give the maximum yield on the investment (Kimes, Barrash, & Alexander, 1999)? Because each seat in the restaurant has a cost, maximizing its use can influence the revenue generated from that seat—this is referred to as seat turnover. If one customer occupies the same seat all evening, the revenue is allocated to just that one person. But maybe it is possible to have two or three people occupying that seat. This is commonly done by moving customers to bars, or to lounge areas for coffee or drinks before and/or after the meal. If the asset of the chair is used by more than one person then the revenue for that chair will increase. The second part, just as in the hotel room, is price variation. This variation of price can be used, for example, when a restaurant has most of its guests arriving between seven and eight in the evening, and it is mostly fully booked, a discount to use the restaurant earlier may help to spread the use of facilities (Sill & Becker, 1999). However, it may be difficult to manage the departure time of the guests, and therefore the handling of meal duration may raise difficult problems for restaurant management. Although at this time little research has been done in this area of yield management, it is evident that it has further implications.

IMPACT ON GUEST SATISFACTION

The impact of yield management on hotel guests is often portrayed in positive terms, in that the guest can experience a reduction in the amount charged for the room. But yield management also has a number of legal and moral issues surrounding its use (Huyton, Evans, & Ingold, 1997; Jones & Hamilton, 1992). The use of yield management in hotel pricing can produce large fluctuations in price, for example, a room that is $100 today may be $150 tomorrow, and these changes can cause dissatisfaction among guests. Management therefore needs to consider ways in which these transitions can be handled, minimizing any dissatisfaction that may occur. This may include the education of guests in the practice of yield management (Kimes, 2004).

In times of drastic reduction in occupancies, accommodation providers undertake various forms of cost cutting to maintain profitability (Arnold, 1994). But reduction must be watched closely to ensure that this process does not affect the quality, both physical as well as the service offered to guests, with this in turn detrimentally impacting occupancy (Stewart, 1994).

The dominance of price as a factor determining occupancy does not seem to take into account the research on the factors that attract guests in the selection of a particular establishment; in fact they seem to represent a management perspective that is devoid of an understanding of the guest. This difference is demonstrated when reviewing literature relating to guest factors affecting selection. Weaver and McCleary's (1991) research indicated that the most important factor affecting the selection of accommodation by business travelers was a clean, comfortable, well-maintained room. Price or room rate was eighteenth in importance as a factor influencing selection of accommodations. Other researchers, Saleh and Ryan (1992), Mehta and Vera (1990), and Lewis (1987), found the same importance as it relates to cleanliness. Recently, research on female business travelers identified an emphasis on cleanliness, appearance, and safety (Shifflet & Bhatia, 1998). The author of this book has also undertaken a number of research projects that have investigated the factors that influence guest selection of accommodations. The question "what are guests looking for in hotel accommodations" is beset by numerous complexities. Much of the previous research gave predetermined lists of attributes and asked for those to be rated. Simply asking a potential guest to rank or indicate in some other way the importance of a number of attributes is inadequate, as this approach does not take into consideration the many factors that influence the decision process, seeming to have focused on the information search stage, and the evaluation of a series of alternatives. As a result there is a fundamental flaw not only in the method of research but also of logic (Lockyer, 2005a). It is of interest that when closed questioning of potential guests is undertaken there is close commonality of results, with cleanliness being identified as the most important factor (Lockyer, 2000, 2002, 2003). However, when focus groups are used for the research other factors such as price become more important (Lockyer, 2005a,b).

In relationship to quality perception, an investigation carried out by Gabor and Granger asked consumers to state the highest and lowest price at which they would purchase selected inexpensive items (Gijsbrechts, 1993). The results of the inquiry allowed the researchers to determine upper and lower price limits for these products based on revealed preference analysis. From the research it is suggested that within these limits price may continue to act as a quality indicator but not as an absolute barrier to purchase. Outside these limits, however, price may act as the dominant indicator of quality and may become a barrier. Price also acts as an indication of quality where if the price is reduced the actual or perceived quality of the establishment can be affected. Therefore, price has an influence on customer expectation and the formation of quality perceptions in a service purchase situation (Lewis & Shoemaker, 1997). When price is used as a dominant indicator of quality, the pricing aspect of the marketing mix can be used to position the product and service offering.

> *In this city there are a lot of promotions around, some even as low as $39.95. How do you cope with the competitive market you are operating in?*
>
> Usually through the service. If they pay $245 or $325, they are not looking for a free breakfast or a bargain. What they are looking for is personal attention, that you personally "recognize me for who I am." If we can get people to come and stay here, we usually "capture" them because we really try and give outstanding service where we personalize. For example for guests staying here for the first time, I will do a nice handwritten card from the manager and I'll attach my business card, and we will send them a gift—it could be a chocolate piano, or cheese and crackers. We track each stay, we have a profile on each guest, so when a guest comes to stay here, when he comes next time we know he likes a foam pillow, he likes his turndown done at 5 o'clock, prefers scotch versus vodka, etc. Each time he comes to stay here we personalize the visit.
>
> (Bruce Fery, General Manager, Grand America, Salt Lake City)

THE INTERNET

In recent times the Internet has changed the way in which guests perceive hotel pricing and how management of a hotel controls yield management practices. Web sites such as "hotels.com" promote themselves as having the "best prices," as do Expedia, Travelocity, Speedy.com, and others.

A major starting point for Internet discounting was in France, where in 2000 the Web site ResHotel was established to offer a system capable of linking hotels and Internet users in real time. It initially had a selection of independent properties and those in lodging chains. The claim made by ResHotel was that it directly links hotels with customers for the price of an Internet connection. The same basic approach to hotel reservations has been implemented by a large number of companies. The strategy followed by many of these sites is to focus to a large extent on the price of the accommodations.

More recently, hotel managers have realized that the use of pricing on the Internet may not be the best approach. One of the main reasons for that is the level of competition that the use of the Internet produces. For example, when a potential guest is looking for accommodations on the Internet they have the ability to tailor the request in a number of different ways, but almost always the user is presented with an array of different hotels with varying prices. At this point the potential guest is very strongly influenced by price, and may not consider other attributes of the hotel, resulting in price becoming the major decision component. It is difficult to measure what impact using the Internet has on the pricing of hotel products (Enz, 2003). Overall, the result has tended to force prices down because price is used as the comparator.

> *It is often said that one of the worst things that the industry did was to expect a discount.*
>
> Yes—(a) to expect discounts and (b) to give the control of their inventory to an outside source. If you don't control your own inventory . . . to companies like Expedia, Travelocity—that you would give your inventory, and they could sell it at what they want. Once you do that you have lost control of your business. 90 percent of the ones that went to it are coming back. At the end of the day there are not a lot of new things to learn about running a business as such. You get new technology and maybe different styles, but the thing that everybody looks for is a fairy godmother to come and save them.
>
> (Terry Holmes, Executive Director,
> The Stafford, London)

To regain control management has developed Web sites to promote their products in their own individual ways, thereby taking the focus away from price. More attractive prices are offered on individual hotel Web sites to attract the prospective customer and promotions and value added features are presented there to encourage the viewer to purchase.

Hotels.com has been a real issue in the United States, how has it changed what you do in managing your pricing strategies?

It has particularly with some of the larger chains; they have really struggled with it because it has become an increasing cost to them, although I am seeing a shift—the cheapest way to get a hotel reservation is through your own Web site, and I am seeing a shift with people trying to sell more of those instead of using Expedia and Travelocity and try to shift them to their Web site where they give them best rate guarantee program, where if you book through the Web site you are given the best rate possible. Everyone is trying to do it. Parity is playing a big role, where everyone is trying to get their rate on par with each other versus the Web site. Companies like us are spending more and more time on Web site development. I have a whole staff—two people—who just work on that every day, making sure our rates are updated, making sure our packages are listed out there, because a lot of people are looking for packages. When someone comes to the nicer hotels or resorts they want to buy a package all inclusive—maybe breakfast, spa—something to attract them. This has the effect that price is not such an issue; the guest perceives the whole package, not just the room cost.

(Bruce Fery, General Manager,
Grand America, Salt Lake City)

Do Web sites such as hotels.com influence what you do?

We have established rate parity with Internet sites and that particular segment of our business (Internet sales) has declined but I think that the customer who wants to come to the Crescent, wants to come to this hotel, and although that particular market segment has decreased we have been able to increase in the other market segments so the rates are higher, better, and the demand has been good enough for us to be able to follow that type of strategy. As a company policy our rates are at parity with what is on the Web site. In our case this works. I think that the typical sophisticated business traveler shops around, certainly ours do perhaps a little, but ultimately they know where they want to go, they know why they want to come here.

(Linda Wan, General Manager,
Hotel Crescent Court, Dallas)

How is your use of the Internet changing?

We are following in the steps of the big companies that are booking business on the Web sites. If you want to get the discounts from the big companies you have to go to the Web sites so we are shifting to that mentality. It is not easy because guests have been trained now to expect and look for discounts. So that is the main concern today. I don't think we can ever maintain control against the very rich marketing companies. They reach out into the market. We are working together, managing our Web site, and offering value to our customers. It is difficult. Of course we have the different kinds of hotel, the 5 diamonds down to the 3 diamonds. In all that there is a great differing knowledge on how to achieve the ends. There are some small companies who do not know what is going on, and they give all they have to Expedia because it is their engine. A company like this one has a different way of looking at that. I am a lot of time involved in this, in order to manage rate, maximize rate and be profitable.

(Luis C. Barrios, General Manager,
Hacienda Hotel Old Town, San Diego)

The Internet is also a source of information for a hotel on the prices being offered by competitors. There are a number of computer packages that automatically search and inquire of Web sites the rate being charged and then this information is correlated into a report to give information on competitive pricing.

What about Internet room-rate-review software?

We use a third party software called Travel-Quick. It electronically searches for prices that are being charged on the Internet for each of the hotels and provides a report.

(William Chu, Director, Revenue Strategy,
Ritz-Carlton Millenia, Singapore)

This sort of software gives revenue managers the ability to evaluate their pricing decisions in relationship to their competitors' practice. Therefore, this represents a valuable resource and one of the important tools in the management of yield.

SUMMARY

Yield management is an easy topic to define but hard to implement. The discussion in this chapter has reviewed the fundamental requirements for the implementation of yield management. Also, decisions on pricing have not only an influence on the day-to-day operation of a property but also can have a much longer-term effect. In many properties room price has become such an important issue that there is a risk that it will become the single most important determinant of the level of occupancy. It is evident from the interviews and other research that such a move is not good for either the individual hotel or for the industry as a whole. By very definition the industry is a service industry and the concepts of service need to be maintained as part of the determinant of occupancy.

Short-term decisions have long-term implications in regard to guest opinions of an establishment, and this influences future purchase behavior. For example, once a guest has been given a discount it is very difficult to not give a discount on the next stay in the hotel.

Yield management is not just related to pricing and giving discounts, it is a way of operating, requiring the support of the whole work force to ensure that the yield of a property is maximized. There is clear evidence that properties are actively working to take back control of their pricing from Internet companies such as hotels.com, and by doing so can add value to their hotels.

The most important issue in any discussion of yield management is monitoring of external events so that those making decisions are making them with a clear understanding of all of the issues that can influence the business in the hotel, and with timely information.

DISCUSSION

A. How can short- and medium-term objectives be in conflict?
B. In considering a number of hotel Internet sites, how do they influence you as a manager, and your decisions?
C. How can staff training influence the profitability of a hotel?
D. What is the relationship between yield management and market segmentation?

E. Imagine you are the hotel manager in a very competitive market and you note that the average room rate for hotels in your area is declining. What action could you take?

F. What level of empowerment would you give your front office staff in setting room rates? (You may wish to review the chapter on empowerment.)

G. Looking at your local hotel industry, what do you see as the most pressing yield management issue?

CASE STUDIES

Case Study 6.1. Management Response to Market Fluctuation

On a year-round basis, in 2004 occupancy was around 75 percent. In the year 2000 it was 89 percent. So occupancies without doubt fell. We hit a peak and didn't know it. Our business is cyclical—we always seem to have five good years and one bad. I think the year 2001 was an all time peak for London and we all felt that it was going to be that way forever. However, even without 9/11 we wouldn't have kept growing—it just couldn't keep getting better every year. As things happen, whether it is a stock market crash or a war, I think you only know how to manage your way through it if you have been there before and made the mistakes already. What happens now in a crisis, the first thing people do is to slash their prices and cut their labor force. If you can charge £500 one day and £200 the next day, there is something not right about what you were doing in the first place. For us, we did not cut our service and we didn't cut our rates because I have seen it before. Those new to hotel management, do that first and yet if you read enough textbooks and speak to enough people, you know it just doesn't work. It takes forever to get back.

Terry Holmes, Executive Director,
The Stafford Hotel, London

Questions

1. How does the business cycle impact yield management?
2. How does long-term planning help to elevate the effect of world crises?
3. Why does inexperienced management cut room rates first?

Case Study 6.2. Desire to Sell

It is very expensive to advertise in the newspaper. I could put up billboards; however, billboards are not very effective because people just get out of the train and walk. Those domestic tourists who come here, they would have a look at the hotel and they would say, "OK I will come back." Then they go to the next hotel, and so on finally choosing between, say, four properties. Actually my selling skills would come in that point. If I am there at the counter with my employees, I have a better chance of selling that room because the employees don't have the same desire and commitment. Secondly, 50 percent of my clients are regulars, they probably come straight to me; they are professionals and they come to the city regularly and they bring their clients, and they know the staff and everybody is friendly to them; staff know their needs. So 50 percent of my clients are all repeat. I have to concentrate on keeping them, making sure they are happy. Price is very competitive. We don't offer discounts. I don't give discounts for one reason—you are a person who comes to stay every week. Also, there is a walk-in customer; in order to sell the room on that particular day I may give a discount. The customer who comes every week is going to say that he has been cheated. People are watching you and you run the risk of losing the regular customers.

P. S. Ramdas, Managing Director,
Tourist Home [Pvt.] Ltd, Egmore, Chennai, India

Questions

1. Why is desire important in yield management?
2. What role does the hotel staff play in yield management?
3. How can managers reduce problems in giving discounts to certain groups of guests?

Case Study 6.3. Relationship Between Business Prosperity and Hotel Yield

Unfortunately in Malaysia we talk less about yield management because it is so competitive, especially after the monetary crisis in the 1990s with the Iraq war, followed by monetary crisis 1996/1997, then we had SARS and economic downturn. A lot of travelers are very cautious about what they are getting in their hotel rooms. We depend on the business market segment. We have very little tourist business. Therefore when industry is affected by monetary crashes a lot of the factories and those in the manufacturing sector either close down or scale down their operations, at the same time they cut down on their traveling expenses and their meeting expenses and that affects us. We don't talk yields. If I charge more the guest says no, other hotel offers me a lower rate. It can even lose a sale for as little as 5 ringgits! (less than US$1.50).

A couple of years back all of the hotels got together to coordinate our approach. We decided not to shock the market too much and decided that 5 star hotels would have nothing below 180 ringgits, 4 star would sell nothing less than 140, 3 star could go around 100. Everybody was happy and shook hands, but it actually worked for about two months. Then customers began to report that other hotels were charging lower, they rang around. So we checked with the General Manager—he looked shocked and passed the buck to Sales Manager. Finally we said ok, it is a free market, do anything you want to do, as long as I keep my hotel full, my staff is happy, they get their salary, they get their service charge, fine. We did try to increase 10 ringgits and straight away you can see your market shifting. And it doesn't matter if occupancy is high or low, you still have to carry the same staff. The trouble is as the rooms deteriorate, if you are not charging enough to maintain the facilities and quality of rooms, over time the quality of the hotel tends to decline and so you charge less. I don't know how tight the market is in New Zealand but here the number of staff is the same whether you have 50 percent or 80 percent. It doesn't matter if occupancy is high or low, you still have to carry the same staff.

Nash Nasihin Ali, General Manager
Mutiara Hotel, Johor, Malaysia

Questions

1. Identify the relationship between room rate and property deterioration in a hotel in your area.
2. Is it ethical or legal for hotel managers to set prices together?
3. How could you better control yield management at times of downturn in the market?

REFERENCES

Arnold, D. (1994). Profits and prices: A lodging analysis. *Cornell Hotel & Restaurant Administration Quarterly, 35*(1), 30-34.

Badinelli, R.D. (2000). An optimal, dynamic policy for hotel yield management. *European Journal of Operational Research, 121*(3), 476.

Berman, B. (2005). Applying yield management pricing to your service business. *Business Horizons, 48*(2), 169.

Brewton, C. (1991). Cutting prices to boost occupancy can be risky. *Hotel & Motel Management, 206*(11), 19-21.

Da Costa, N. (2001). Differential pricing and segmentation on the internet: The case of hotels. *Management Decision, 39*(4), 252-262.

Ellerbrock, M.J., Hite, J.C., & Wells, G. (1984). Competition and lodging room rates. *International Journal of Hospitality Management, 3*(1), 11-18.

Enz, C.A. (2003). Hotel pricing in a networked world. *Cornell Hotel and Restaurant Administration Quarterly, 44*(1), 4-6.

Feiertag, H. (1992). Discounting rates does more harm than good. *Hotel & Motel Management, 207*(18), 14.

Gijsbrechts, E. (1993). Prices and pricing research in consumer marketing: Some recent developments. *International Journal of Research in Marketing, 10*(2), 115-151.

Higley, J. (2003). Discounting isn't bad when it's done correctly. *Hotel and Motel Management, 218*(13), 8.

Huyton, J., Evans, P., & Ingold. (1997). The legal and moral issues surrounding the practise of yield management. *International Journal of Contemporary Hospitality Management, 9*(2), 84-87.

Jones, P. (1999). Yield management in UK hotels: A systems analysis. *The Journal of the Operational* Research *Society, 50*(11), 1111-1119.

Jones, P., & Hamilton, D.H. (1992). Yield management: Putting people in the big picture. *Cornell Hotel and Restaurant Administration Quarterly, 30*(1), 89-95.

Kimes, S.E. (1999). Implementing restaurant revenue management. *Cornell Hotel and Restaurant Administration Quarterly, 40*(3), 16-21.

Kimes, S.E. (2004). Restaurant revenue management: Implementation at Chevys Arrowhead. *Cornell Hotel and Restaurant Administration Quarterly, 45*(1), 52-68.

Kimes, S.E., Barrash, D.I., & Alexander, J.E. (1999). Developing a restaurant revenue-management strategy. *Cornell Hotel and Restaurant Administration Quarterly, 40*(5), 18-30.

Koide, T., & Ishii, H. (2005). The hotel yield management with two types of room prices, overbooking and cancellation. *International Journal of Production Economics, 93-94*, 417.

Koss, L. (1992). Room-rate structures simplified. *Hotel & Motel Management, 207*(7), 84-85.

Ladany, S.P. (2001). Optimal hotel segmentation mix strategy. *International Journal of Services Technology and Management, 2*(1/2), 18.

Lewis, R.C. (1987). The measurement of gaps in the quality of hotel services. *International Journal of Hospitality Management, 6*(2), 83-88.

Lewis, R.C., & Shoemaker, S. (1997). Price-sensitivity measurement: A tool for the hospitality industry. *Cornell Hotel & Restaurant Administration Quarterly, 38*(2), 44-47.

Lieberman, W.H. (1993). Debunking the myths of yield management. *Cornell Hotel and Restaurant Administration Quarterly, 34*(1), 34-41.

Lockyer, T. (2000). A New Zealand investigation into the factors influencing consumers' selection of business hotel accommodation. *Australian Journal of Hospitality Management, 7*(2), 11-23.

Lockyer, T. (2002). Business guests accommodation selection: The view from both sides. *International Journal of Contemporary Hospitality Management, 14*(6), 294-300.

Lockyer, T. (2003). Hotel cleanliness: How do guests view it? Let's get specific. *The International Journal of Hospitality Management, 22*(3), 297-305.

Lockyer, T. (2005a). The perceived importance of price as one hotel selection dimension. *Tourism Management, 26*(5), 529-537.

Lockyer, T. (2005b). Understanding the dynamics of the hotel purchase decision. *International Journal of Contemporary Hospitality Management, 17*(6), 529-537.

Marshall, A. (1995). It doesn't take a fool to spy erratic pricing. *Hotel & Motel Management, 210*(7), 24.

Mehta, S.C., & Vera, A. (1990). Segmentation in Singapore. *Cornell Hotel and Restaurant Administration Quarterly, 30*(1), 80-87.

Morley, C.L. (1994). Discrete choice analysis of the impact of tourism price. *Journal of Tourism Research, 33*(2), 8-14.

Mullen, M. (1998). Rules of thumb: Help or hindrance? (UK). *Accountancy, March,* 59-60.

Okumus, F. (2004). Implementation of yield management practices in service organizations: Empirical findings from a major hotel group. *The Service Industry Journal, 24*(6), 65-74.

Overby, S. (2005). The price is always right; Marriott applied its business wisdom to building an IT system that has successfully tackled its greatest challenge—Maximizing revenue. *CIO. Framingham, 18*(9), 1.

Saleh, F., & Ryan, C. (1992). Client perceptions of hotels, a multi-attribute approach. *Tourism, (3),* 163-168.

Shaw, M. (1992). Positioning and price: Merging theory, strategy, and tactics. *Hospitality Research Journal, 15*(2), 31-39.

Shifflet, D.K., & Bhatia, P. (1998). Hotels must change to meet needs of female travellers. *Hotel and Motel Management, 213*(16), 32.

Sill, B., & Becker, R. (1999). Applying capacity-management science: The case of browns restaurant. *Cornell Hotel and Restaurant Administration Quarterly, 40*(3), 22-30.

Smith, B.C., Leimkubler, J.F., & Darrow, R.M. (1992). Yield management at American Airlines. *Interfaces, 22*(1), 8-31.

Stewart, B.A. (1994). From chapter 11 to profitability. *Bottom-Line, 9*(4), 16-17.

Weaver, P.A., & McCleary, K.W. (1991). Basics bring 'em back: Extras are appreciated, but business travellers still value good service and good management. *Hotel and Motel Management, June 24,* 29-30, 32, 38.

Zeithaml, V.A., & Bitner, M.J. (1996). *Service Marketing.* New York: McGraw Hill.

Chapter 7

Sustainability

Sustainability is especially ripe for political controversy and opposition because fundamentally it is a new paradigm that represents significant challenges to the status quo. The paradigm of sustainability, with its notions of limitations and carrying capacities confronts dominant paradigms of progress which do not recognize limits to unchecked growth.

Hazel Henderson, Economist

CHAPTER OBJECTIVES

On completion of this chapter the reader will understand

- the importance of sustainability in today's hotel industry
- the way in which the various topics of this book come together in a sustainable management relationship
- the ways in which different management principles influence sustainability
- the importance of planning for a business to be sustainable
- the ways in which sustainability influences a hotel's profitability
- the delicate balance that a hotel operates under

The International Hotel Industry: Sustainable Management
© 2007 by The Haworth Press, Inc. All rights reserved.
doi:10.1300/5869_08

Key Word Definitions

cyclical: Recurring or revolving in circles.

ecological health: The occurrence of certain attributes that are deemed to be present in a healthy, sustainable resource.

economic success: The ability of a hotel to survive economically in an interrelated environment.

social responsibility: Occurs when a hotel acts in the best interests of society, as well as its own profit motive, by balancing corporate citizenship with a fair level of profits.

vulnerable: Capable of being physically wounded or hurt; susceptible to attack.

Chapter Review

This chapter is perhaps the most important of all and has been left till last to allow theories to be explored and grasped so that the reader is prepared for what must be the underlying focus of all—true sustainability of the business.

This chapter provides a brief discussion of sustainability and then gives an insight into its application and importance within the hotel industry.

INTRODUCTION TO THEORY: SUSTAINABILITY

In 1987, the World Commission on Environment and Development (WCED) introduced the term "sustainable development" and it has been defined as "development which meets the needs of the present without compromising the ability of future generations to meet their own needs." There have been a number of authors (Holmberg, 1992; Pearce, Barbier, & Markandyn, 1990; Reid, 1995) who have helped with the interpretation of the original WCED report and have assisted with a wider understanding of what sustainability means in a modern environment.

Sustainability is becoming an important focus being directly related to the resources available and how those resources are used today and how they will be used in the future. The concepts and application of sustainability are an important component in the management of any business. Humankind has reached a point in the history of the world where it needs to rethink where it is going and how it is going to get there. In many respects, over the past 350 years, humans have built their hopes and dreams for progress on the concept of unlimited economic growth. This thought has led to the belief that more production and consumption is good, regardless of the impacts of these actions in areas such as the environment and society. However, there is a vital relationship between continual growth and available resources and the future which requires serious consideration. At the heart of the decisions that have guided businesses for the past 350 years is the image of the economy being a closed circular flow. In this the resources are transformed by businesses into products and services that are purchased by consumers. Such a model is isolated from many of the social impacts, see Figure 7.1.

EXTERNAL INFLUENCES ON A HOTEL AND SUSTAINABILITY

Within the hospitality industry there are many ways in which to talk about sustainability including, for example, recycling napkins, the use of energy saving light bulbs, or the use of energy produced in the kitchen to heat a hotel's water. While these measures can assist in some small ways, and are often more profit motivated than sustainability motivated, a much wider view is required. In this book, the concept of sustainability flows through and is part of everything that happens in a hotel. Sustainable management is not about how managers do things to try and make a business more sustainable, it is how

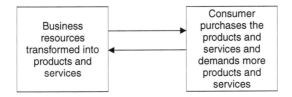

FIGURE 7.1. Closed Economic Flow

the managers view the business and the environment in which the business operates. As management in a hotel think about the day-to-day operations, long-term financial viability, and the employees, along with other resources, all of these need to be evaluated in a sustainable way. Figure 7.2 illustrates the relationship of the elements of the model of interrelationship.

MANAGEMENT DECISIONS AND IMPACT ON SUSTAINABILITY

As shown in Figure 7.2 the six areas covered in this book are illustrated connecting together in an environment of economic success, social responsibility, and ecological health (Daub & Ergenzinger, 2005; Gupta, McDaniel, & Herath, 2005). These are not the only elements

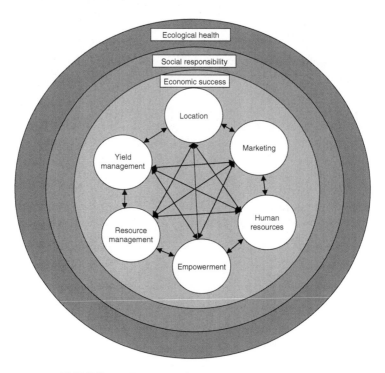

FIGURE 7.2. Elements of the Model of Sustainability

that management needs to consider but it does give some indication of the importance of each element in a connected environment. Sustainability cannot be considered in isolation, it needs to involve all the stakeholders of the hotel. This includes the guests, employees, suppliers, competitors, owners, investors, local and national councils, governments, and so on—in fact all those who have an interest in the continued operation of the hotel. Each chapter in this book aims toward promoting sustainability and the long term success of the business. As an example, in the chapter on yield management, it is possible to have maximum occupancy percentages as a primary goal. Internationally there are examples of companies who do that, but without consideration that the many factors which interconnect could lead to an unsustainable situation. The short-term gain may be high, but unless consideration is given to such areas as the depreciation of the property, the employees, the facilities, and the impact that high occupancy has on them, this objective may not be sustainable.

Changes in a market can have a profound impact on a hotel. External changes to a market which may be uncontrollable by the individual hotel can have flow-on effect and impact the mix of the accommodations available so all providers are influenced. Some of the issues that are important to sustainability were discussed with the senior management within the industry during the interviews. These interviews revealed some very interesting issues, especially those conducted in Spain. Some of the questions posed are included here as they show examples of the interconnectivity that the elements have on a hotel.

How has your market changed in relation to sustainable business practices?

Traditionally we were the upmarket area here—Marbeja always had the finest hotels, the finest restaurants, they always had the facilities for the upmarket visit. Already this year we can see very clearly that type of upmarket customer somehow is slowly disappearing and hotels are having to replace them with a different type of customer. There are two negatives here—number one, you are losing prime profit; number two, where you were practically alone, you had your competitor in Mediterranean, Sardinia, and the more exclusive resorts in the French Riviera. Now if you go below in the market you have to compete with everybody. It is a no-win situation.

(Rafael de la Fuente, Director Gerente,
Escuela De Hosteleria, Benalmedena Pueblo, Spain)

As illustrated, changes in the market are placing hotels in a vulnerable situation. This is not just a marketing problem—the market as a whole is changing and that is affecting the sustainability of the whole market, not simply the profitability of hotels. The susceptibility of hotels to external factors is also illustrated from the following extract about Torremolinos, which shows similarities to what is beginning to happen in Marbeja. What is important to reflect on in both situations is the impact that management decisions have during such a decline in a market, and if better decision making at an earlier time may have changed the outcome.

> *What lessons could managers learn about the vulnerability of the hotel industry?*
>
> In the late fifties and early sixties Torremolinos was the most fashionable place in Spain. Torremolinos had a concentration of six super quality hotels within a fairly small area. They also had the greatest concentration of fine restaurants, boutiques, and all the amenities geared to a benevolent kind of tourism. At the same time it became very quickly a very strong tourist destination in southern Europe—it was like a miracle. At that time Spain was emerging from a long postwar period. The war had finished 10-15 years before that. It was incredible because there were nonstop flights from major European cities but very quickly it was spoiled and destroyed. Then Torremolinos became a symbol known not for excellence, not as a very high quality, sophisticated tourist resort but just the opposite—atrocious buildings all over the place. Some of those hotels of the old days still exist but are a shadow of what they once were. The clientele in a very short space of time, maybe couple of years, just moved somewhere else. We already have had an experience but we don't seem to have learned from it.
>
> (Rafael de la Fuente, Director Gerente,
> Escuela De Hosteleria, Benalmedena Pueblo, Spain)

HOTELS AND SOCIAL SUSTAINABILITY

Hotels and the environment in which they operate change continually throughout the world and clearly some follow a ruinous course. In the chapter on yield management there was a discussion on the impact that price can have on a property's continued operation. In the following extract other stakeholders become more evident particularly concerning the interaction with other parties in the sustained operation of the hotel.

Why is a sustainable view important to management?

I see so many times in the Canary Islands and Ozores: when you open a hotel and you have a debit in the bank of 50 million Euros and you have to pay 200 staff every month; there are social security costs and water, and power, and insurance, and so on and you don't have a good cash flow or a big solid company behind you, so you start selling very cheap. Two things happen: you have to sell every day more cheaply— so you can't give the good service and the good food and every day you get less customers. The bank says you have to pay me interest, or we sell. So every day you owe them more.

(Rafael de la Fuente, Director Gerente,
Escuela De Hosteleria, Benalmedena Pueblo, Spain)

As previously discussed in the chapter on human resource management, staffing is one of the most pressing issues within hotels. There are many demands placed on employees that can influence the quality of the hotel, and thus influence customer satisfaction (Daub & Ergenzinger, 2005). Generally, around the world there seems a reluctance among young people to enter the industry. The following are two excellent examples of innovative ways to influence the perception of the industry and give it a better social image.

What actions are being taken to influence potential staff and society's view of the hotel industry?

To try and develop the accommodation business and to encourage and educate potential recruits, we have developed a proactive approach. The scheme has produced some really good results. Because some of the research suggested that our local children won't go into the industry because they will do a week's work experience in a hotel, have a terrible experience, and come out saying that is the last time I will ever darken the door of a hotel. So we worked with the schoolchildren to produce a work experience pack where the children have a copy and the hotel has a copy. The hotel doesn't have to think about or work hard at it, they just implement it. It is a nice simple checklist approach. The child gets a better quality experience, a much more varied experience, and is much more inclined to want to come back and enter the industry.

(Christine Collier, Managing Director,
Cumbria Tourist Board, Cumbria, England)

The cyclical changes that have an impact on hotels flow through all parts of society. The employment of staff is not simply a factor of availability, it is also influenced by other opportunities available to the potential employees.

Are there sufficient staff for the industry locally?

In this area where there is a tremendous building boom going on, a lot of young people have decided to work in the building industry because they can get much more money, the hours are easier, and so on. But the amount of money they receive and their very jobs are not for the long term because when these buildings are finished, a lot of young workers will try to go back to the hospitality industry and then the problem will be their lack of training. Highly skilled and trained people right now are being extremely well paid compared to other professions. Chefs and waiters are being offered some very good salaries and splendid working conditions.

(Rafael de la Fuente, Director Gerente,
Escuela De Hosteleria, Benalmadena Pueblo, Spain)

These examples were chosen because of their graphic illustration of the ways in which the hotel industry is influenced by external factors. The keen reader will look around at his or her local area and identify examples with resounding similarities.

SUMMARY

There are two distinct but highly related considerations regarding sustainability. The first is the sustainability for stakeholders of the successful hotel business. The second is the overarching consideration of sustainability for the planet and the future. This chapter has tried to bring together some of the factors that influence a hotel's operations from not only within but also outside the hotel. As you review each of the previous chapters, although they could be considered as discrete and the management of the issues likewise, as is evident from Figure 7.1, that is too simplistic an approach. For a hotel to operate successfully it must be managed in a sustainable way so that a balanced approach is taken. Hotels use large amounts of energy, natural human resources and have impacts on society which need consideration from a holistic view.

DISCUSSION

A. Evaluate hotel location in a sustainable business environment. Identify local and international issues that influence such an environment.
B. Evaluate hotel marketing in a sustainable business environment. What are the influences on such an environment?
C. Evaluate hotel human resources in a sustainable business environment. Identify local and international issues that influence such an environment.
D. Evaluate hotel empowerment in a sustainable business environment. Identify local and international issues that influence such an environment.
E. Evaluate hotel resource management in a sustainable business environment. Identify local and international issues that influence such an environment.
F. Evaluate hotel yield management in a sustainable business environment. Identify local and international issues that influence such an environment.
G. Draw up an active plan of how your management style will influence sustainability.

REFERENCES

Daub, C.H., & Ergenziner, R. (2005). Enabling sustainable management through a new multi-disciplinary concept of customer satisfaction. *European Journal of Marketing, 39*(9/10), 998-1015.

Gupta, A., McDaniel, J.C., & Herath, S.K. (2005). Quality management in service firms: Sustaining structures of total quality service. *Managing Service Quality, 15*(4), 389-402.

Holmberg, Johan, Ed. (1992). *Making development sustainable.* Washington, DC: Island Press.

Pearce, D., Barbier, E., & Markandyn, A. (1990). *Sustainable development: Economics and environment in the third world.* London: Earthscan.

Reid, D. (1995). *Sustainable development: An introductory guide.* London: Earthscan.

Index

Page numbers followed by the letter "f" indicate figures and those followed by the letter "e" indicate exhibits.